JOHN PAUL II

A TRIBUTE IN WORDS AND PICTURES

JOHN PAUL II

A TRIBUTE IN WORDS AND PICTURES

MONSIGNOR VIRGILIO LEVI AND
CHRISTINE ALLISON

WILLIAM MORROW
An Imprint of HarperCollins*Publishers*

Library of Congress Cataloging-in-Publication Data
has been applied for.

ISBN 0-688-16621-0

Printed in the United States of America

First Edition

2 3 4 5 6 7 8 9 10

BOOK DESIGN BY CHARLES KRELOFF

www.williammorrow.com

FOR WICK

PREFACE

It is questionable whether there can ever be too many books written about Pope John Paul II. This is a man of such depth, of so many facets, of such an intriguing personality, of so unlikely a background that no author, no multiplicity of authors could ever present the totality.

One of the charms of *Pope John Paul II: A Tribute in Words and Pictures* is that the authors, Monsignor Virgilio Levi and Christine Allison, do not attempt to exhaust their subject or provide a definitive portrayal. Their work serves as a gentle reminder of the great value of understatement.

At the same time, the straightforward writing is both refreshing and provocative. To say, for example, that by the time of Pope John Paul II's second trip to Poland, in 1983, "The Poles were worn to the bone," speaks volumes of what awaited him upon his arrival. Their resistance, the authors note, "was fragmented and dispirited." The prisons bulged with political dissidents, "many of them the pope's protégés." One such as myself, not personally involved in either visit, has to be amazed at the difference in our Holy Father's own country in the short period from 1979 to 1983. However, once again, this pope would not be intimidated. As a result, the Poles overflowed Czestochowa, to see and to hear him. This second visit was the occasion on which he validated the magic word that he used over and over again: SOLIDARITY!

The account of Karol Wojtyla's childhood and youth is warm and gentle without becoming at any time unduly sentimental. This was a young boy, a young man, who obviously knew who he was from a very early age. As one who has had the privilege on many occasions of face-to-face meetings with John Paul II, and of luncheons with him in his own dining room, I find this to be perhaps his most striking characteristic: he knows exactly who he is at all times and under all circumstances. Far more than merely *writing* about phenomenological personalism, his own philosophical bent, he clearly considers the individual with whom he is speaking or to whom he is listening at any given moment the most important individual in the whole world. In my view, that is phenomenological personalism brought to life.

The authors have provided a further service by periodically citing portions of this man's most beautiful poetry. Equally poetic, however, is their brief but pungent coverage of visit after visit Pope John Paul II has made throughout the world—pungent because in but a few sentences they give us a sense of the truly remarkable changes that take place even before, but specifically because of, his pending visit to a given land. So, for example, Philippines president Marcos felt it imperative to relax martial law because of the pope's forthcoming visit.

The clarity in the text of *A Tribute in Words and Pictures* is paralleled by the poignancy of the pictures. Readers will linger over them time after time with keen delight. The text, too, will be read and reread. As one who has devoured a great number of works on this pope for whom I have unashamed affection and love, I express my personal and deep gratitude to the authors of this particular work, who clearly share my sentiments for their subject.

—JOHN CARDINAL O'CONNOR
ARCHBISHOP OF NEW YORK
APRIL 1999

PRAYER OF HIS HOLINESS POPE JOHN PAUL II FOR THE GREAT JUBILEE OF THE YEAR 2000

l. Blessed are you, Father,
who, in your infinite love,
gave us your only-begotten Son.
By the power of the Holy Spirit he became incarnate
in the spotless womb of the Virgin Mary
and was born in Bethlehem
two thousand years ago.

He became our companion on life's path
and gave new meaning to our history,
the journey we make together
in toil and suffering,
in faithfulness and love,
towards the new heaven and the new earth
where You, once death has been vanquished, will be all in all.

Praise and glory to You, Most Holy Trinity,
you alone are God most high!

2. By your grace, O Father, may the Jubilee Year
be a time of deep conversion
and of joyful return to you.
May it be a time of reconciliation between people,
and of peace restored among nations,
a time when swords are beaten into ploughshares
and the clash of arms gives way to songs of peace.

Father, grant that we may live this Jubilee Year
docile to the voice of the Spirit,
faithful to the way of Christ,
diligent in listening to your Word
and in approaching the wellsprings of grace.

Praise and glory to You, most Holy Trinity,
you alone are God most high!

3. Father, by the power of the Spirit,
strengthen the Church's commitment to the new
  evangelization
and guide our steps along the pathways of the world,
to proclaim Christ by our lives,

and to direct our earthly pilgrimage
towards the City of heavenly light.

May Christ's followers show forth their love
for the poor and the oppressed;
may they be one with those in need
and abound in works of mercy;
may they be compassionate towards all,
that they themselves may obtain indulgence and
forgiveness from you.

Praise and glory to You, Most Holy Trinity,
you alone are God most high!

4. Father, grant that your Son's disciples
purified in memory
and acknowledging their failings,
may be one, that the world may believe.
May dialogue between the followers of the great religions
  prosper,
and may all people discover the joy of being your children.

May the intercession of Mary, Mother of your faithful people,
in union with the prayers of the Apostles, the Christian
  martyrs,
and the righteous of all nations in every age,
make the Holy Year a time of renewed hope and of joy in the
  Spirit
for each of us and for the whole Church.

Praise and glory to You, Most Holy Trinity,
you alone are God most high!

5. To you, Almighty Father, Creator of the universe and of
  mankind,
through Christ, the Living One, Lord of time and history,
in the Spirit who makes all things holy,
be praise and honour and glory
now and for ever. Amen!

—JOHN PAUL II

ACKNOWLEDGMENTS

At the end of my modest work, I want to express my humble thanks to Almighty God, the Father, the Son, and the Holy Spirit, the Lord of history, Creator and Enlightener of every human mind. Then, to the memory of Their Holinesses Pope Paul VI and Pope John Paul I, and TO HIS HOLINESS POPE JOHN PAUL II, WHO HAVE GIVEN ME THE PRIVILEGE OF SERVING THEM AT THE VATICAN. Lastly, to Their Holy Eminences Camillo Cardinal Ruini, Vicar of Rome, and John Joseph Cardinal O'Connor, Archbishop of New York, and to Their Excellencies Archbishops Giovanni Battista Re and Carlo Maria Viganó, of the Secretariat of State of His Holiness, and Renato Raffaele Martino, Permanent Observer of the Holy See to the United Nations, for their important and kind help.

I also would like to warmly thank the following people:

Carla Morselli, photographer, for her professional skill and availability

Dominick Morawski, Polish-Italian international journalist, for his kind assistance in checking Polish names and history

The principal editors of the Vatican newspaper *L'Osservatore Romano,* an authoritative source of information on the history and life of the contemporary Church and the Roman Pontiffs: Professor Mario Agnes, editor-in-chief of the daily international edition, and Reverend Monsignor Robert J. Dempsey, responsible for the weekly edition in English

Eminent university professors and head physicians Attilio Maseri, cardiologist; Gian Federico Possati, heart surgeon; Stefano Maria Zuccaro, gerontologist; and also my eldest sister, Professor Rosanna Levi, living with me in Rome, who enabled me to edit this book at a time when I was experiencing some health problems.

—MONSIGNOR VIRGILIO LEVI
ROME AND VATICAN CITY
25 MARCH 1999
SOLEMNITY OF THE ANNUNCIATION

This book was a collaboration of love. Our intention was to create a simple book, not a definitive biography or photographic study but a book through which one might become acquainted with a very complex and holy man. The book is infused with the love of Monsignor Levi, who dedicated his full intellect and spirit and enthusiasm to editing this brief volume. Under any circumstances his devotion would have been remarkable, but in fact he toiled under the duress of "urgent American deadlines," while in an extremely fragile physical state. His poor health did not stand in the way of his determination to be faithful and accurate—and also to keep all parties calm and in excellent cheer. Any errors or lapses in language or intelligence are my own. Mille grazie, Don Levi. I love you.

Besides Monsignor Levi and those esteemed individuals whom he has mentioned, I would like to thank those whose prayers and presence gave me the ability to work on this book, especially my husband, Wick, and my children, Gillea, Maisie, Chrissie, and Loddie. Lupe Morales. Jenny Lea Allison. Marie and John Peterson. Ginny and David Bauer. Barbara Krueger. Karen Goodwin. Ginny Dominick Kelly. Mickie Teetor. Michael Lavalle. St. Teresa of Avila. Jack. Anita Middleton. Patty Brown. John Boswell. Amy Handy. Charles Kreloff. My editor and fellow Valkyrie, Meaghan Dowling. All holy priests and nuns and monks, especially Father George Weber. And to my godchildren, Nicholas, Alison, and Callie, may the peace of Christ be with you.

—CHRISTINE ALLISON
DALLAS, TEXAS
6 APRIL 1999

CONTENTS

JOHN PAUL II

A TRIBUTE IN WORDS
AND PICTURES

POLAND

———⊰⊱———

1920 TO 1942

Deus, docuisti me a iuventute mea;
et usque nunc annuntiabo mirabilia tua.

*(God, you have taught me from my youth. And
even now I proclaim your wondrous works.)*

—Psalm 71:17

GROWING UP IN WADOWICE

In a Polish village called Wadowice, just down from the cobbled town square, stands an unremarkable two-story apartment house. On the basis of its architecture it would seem an unlikely stop for a tour bus. Yet every year, from all over the world, nearly two hundred thousand visitors make the pilgrimage to 7 Church Street, to view the place where Karol Wojtyla (pronounced Voy-te-wah) spent his childhood.

There is little to see. A kitchen and two rooms. Some primitive-looking sporting equipment. The "tour" is an abbreviated, even disappointing affair if you are searching for clues about the childhood of the twentieth century's most powerful pope. You make your way down the stairs and hurry out of the musty building for fresh air. Then you look up, and see it: the Church of Our Lady of Perpetual Help.

Every day, for the whole of his childhood, little Karol Wojtyla scrambled down the stairs and out the door and ran into . . . the Catholic Church. Next door to his unremarkable house was God's house. God and man had lived this way in Poland for nearly a thousand years. Ninety-nine percent of all Poles are baptized Catholic. Until the 1900s Latin was the language of official business. The Poles are so identified with Catholicism that they view themselves as protectors of the Church, even as its white knight.

But in recent centuries Poland could not even protect itself. With its indefensible shoreline and uncommonly flat terrain, Poland was a political sitting duck. Since 1772 the country has been overrun, partitioned, and nearly obliterated by Prussia, Austria, Russia, Nazi Germany, and the Soviet Union. But even with the Polish nation dismembered, Polish nationhood survived. Foreign occupation became the catalyst for a Polish renaissance, especially in literature, art, and drama. Clinging to the memories of previous generations, Poles told stories about their own warriors and saints. Every schoolchild knew about Queen Jadwiga, who married a Lithuanian and in so doing enlarged the Polish empire, and St. Stanislaw, the bishop who defied a despotic king. Over the years, the names of these heroic Poles became a kind of political shorthand that recalled ancient glories to a people burdened by modern tyrannies.

4

While Polish literature and arts blossomed, religion moved center stage. In their Catholicism, Poles found not only sanctuary, but hope. However their country had been divided, the sound of church bells could still cross any border, and the bells rang out, helping Poles to remember who they were.

After World War I, when the Allies defeated Germany and Austro-Hungary, Poland found its opening and made a worldwide case for its freedom. In 1919, with the signing of the Versailles Treaty, Poland regained its independence.

A year later, into the new, modern Poland, Karol Wojtyla was born.

NUMBER 7 CHURCH STREET

No. 7 Church Street: *The Wojtylas rented the second floor of this building, located in the village of Wadowice, just off the town square. Every year nearly 200,000 people visit the pope's birthplace, searching for clues about the most influential pope of this century.*

Looking back to 7 Church Street, there was little in Karol Wojtyla's childhood to suggest that he might be destined for greatness. His parents, Karol Wojtyla, Sr., and Emilia Kaczorowska, were decent working people, both originally from a southwestern province called Galicja. The Wojtylas were essentially working class; the Kaczorowskis were of a loftier, bourgeois lineage. Though hardly nobility, Emilia's family discouraged her from seeing Karol, and were dead set against her "marrying down." But Emilia prevailed, and married Karol in 1906. He was twenty-six, she was twenty-one.

In the eyes of the world, the Wojtylas were not particularly distinguished. Karol Sr. was a low-level career officer in the military, basically a clerk. And he had the temperament of a clerk: calm and dedicated, if somewhat uncommunicative. His army file acknowledges his ample strengths of character and his fluency in the Polish and German languages, but his skills fell mainly into the category of "fast typist." Emilia was a former school teacher and had been the beneficiary of a convent education. She later took in sewing to supplement the family's household income. She is recalled as a good-natured woman.

Until Poland gained its independence, the Wojtylas lived in Krakow on a meager stipend from Karol Sr.'s former employment in the Austrian military. Into their modest but cheerful home a first child, Edmund, was born in 1906. Six years later, Emilia gave birth to a little girl, Olga, who died in infancy. Olga's mysterious death devastated the Wojtylas; Emilia in particular seems never fully to have recovered from the loss.

With the formation of modern Poland, an army was hastily organized; Karol Sr. joined and was elevated to lieutenant in the 12th regiment. This meant a minor increase in his income and a transfer from Krakow to the small town of Wadowice, some thirty miles southwest. A year later, on May 18, 1920, Karol Jozef Wojtyla—nicknamed Lolek—was born, and was baptized a month later by the Reverend Franciszek Zak at the Wadowice church. Lolek's godfather was one of Emilia's brothers-in-law, Jozef Kuczmierczyk, and his godmother was Emilia's sister, Maria Wiadrowska.

Faded photographs from the 1920s show Lolek as a handsome child who, like Edmund, resembled his mother. He casts a curiously mature gaze into the lens, and is mostly garbed in the dresses worn by European boys his age. He is frequently pictured with his father. The

KALWARIA ZEBRZYDOWSKA

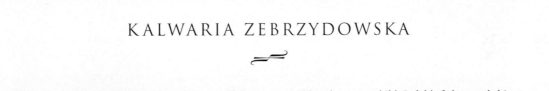

Long before Lolek was born, his grandfather and his great-grandfather served as guides at a Bernardine Fathers monastery called Kalwaria Zebrzydowska. Located several miles from Wadowice, it has a wooded path that recalls Via Dolorosa, the road of suffering, where Christ walked the Stations of the Cross. The Stations of the Cross depict Christ's procession to death on the cross. They are represented in Catholic churches throughout the world, replicated in Rome just outside the Colosseum on Good Friday each year, and of course enshrined in Jerusalem. Generally, there are fourteen stations; at Kalwaria, the experience of walking with Christ on this sorrowful journey is intensified by the presence of dozens of stops over five miles of trail.

When he was a child, Lolek's father took him to Kalwaria. After his mother's funeral, Lolek came to Kalwaria to weep, finally letting go after holding in his grief. When Lolek became a priest, he took his students to Kalwaria for long walks and conversations and silence. As archbishop, Wojtyla would actually schedule meetings there, then take long walks, hours at a time, alone. When Pope Paul VI named Wojtyla a cardinal, he came to Kalwaria before boarding the plane to Rome. Inscribed in the guest book is this statement: "I came to Our Lady of Kalwaria, to whom I have felt close since my childhood, to put everything in her hands." Kalwaria, like God, had been one of the few constants in Wojtyla's life.

On June 7, 1979, Wojtyla returned to Kalwaria, as Pope John Paul II.

FAMILY PORTRAIT: *With Emilia's frail health, Karol Wojtyla, Sr., was virtually a single parent. A career soldier who was nicknamed "The Lieutenant," he was rarely seen out of uniform. Lolek and his father lived on a small military pension for most of their lives together.*

detail reveals much: a protective arm, a lightly held hand; Karol Sr., who was known as a strict disciplinarian, also appears to have been quite tender with his youngest son. Emilia is portrayed less often in family photographs. Her health was deteriorating steadily and doubtless her heart condition precluded much portraiture.

Still, life in Wadowice had its own lyrical pace, and the Wojtylas seemed content. Though they had little money, most of the best entertainment was free; there were hills, mountains, lakes, and rivers ideal for picnics and sports. Lolek attended an overcrowded public school on the second floor of a municipal building. Recess was on the street in front of the Wadowice church, and it was there that Lolek learned to play soccer. The boy was a conscientious student, generally making the American equivalent of straight As.

As a young child, Lolek knew his mother suffered from a degenerative illness. Though he was probably unaware of the specifics, he knew that if it was a "good day" she might be able to visit for a few minutes. Otherwise she would be in bed, needing "silence." Often she was not even home but off in Krakow in search of medical treatment. Like most Poles, she was tightlipped about her suffering.

After just a few years, Edmund went off to Jagiellonian University in Krakow to study medicine. From that point forward, Lolek was raised with the attention and focus usually devoted to an only child, and with Emilia's worsening condition, he was largely under the supervision and guidance of his father. Everyone in Wadowice affectionately called Karol Sr. "The Lieutenant," which was as much a reference to his personality as to his rank. Karol Sr. ran the Wojtyla household with a penchant for order. His father's regimented approach, though a bit starched, apparently served to provide an enormous sense of stability for Lolek.

Lolek's father operated with military efficiency but he was also a deeply spiritual man. He transmitted his love of God to Lolek not so much through catechesis, but by the way he lived. The Wojtylas were like most Catholic Poles; their home contained the symbols of their faith—crucifixes, a painting of the Blessed Mary, and holy water in a vessel by the door. Lolek wore the scapular he received at First Communion every single day (and still wears it, seventy years later). But faith in the Wojtyla home went deeper: it was embodied in the

THE BAPTISMAL FONT: *The future pope was baptized on June 20, 1920, by Reverend Franciszek Zak, a military chaplain, in the Wadowice church Our Lady of Perpetual Help. The baptismal font and candle are shown here.*

11

THE BLACK MADONNA

In the summer of 1932, twelve-year-old Lolek went with a church tour group to a village called Czestochowa, a medieval city that draws pilgrims from all over Poland, there to see the damaged but hauntingly beautiful painted image of the Blessed Virgin. Once inside the ancient village, the faithful proceed down the main street and then climb Jasna Gora (Clear Hill) ever upward, until they reach a fourteenth-century monastery. Inside the monastery is the Polish national treasure they came so far to see, a painting called the Black Madonna.

Legends about the Black Madonna abound. A popular notion holds that the painting is the work of the Evangelist Luke, and that the painting itself is rendered on a piece of the wooden table from Christ's home as a child. The painting itself was torn by a Hussite group in 1430, but it was never repaired, bearing the wounds instead, which actually give the appearance of tears running down the face of the Madonna.

In 1966 the primate of Poland, Cardinal Stefan Wyszynski, concluded the "Great Novena" (nine years of spiritual preparation) honoring the one thousandth anniversary of the coming of Christianity to Poland. The culmination of the nine-year observances was an open-air Mass on Easter Sunday held in the vast area facing the shrine of the Blessed Black Madonna, con-celebrated by Cardinal Wyszynski and Cardinal Wojtyla.

More than a decade later, Pope John Paul II gathered millions at Czestochowa, rallying the Poles at one of the lowest moments of the Soviet occupation. His bold proclamation, "Solidarity, solidarity," a term then banned from Poland, fueled the hearts and souls of his people.

The Black Madonna is very dear to John Paul's heart. When he became pope, he asked that her image be set above the altar in his private chapel.

AVE MARIA: *The future pope revered the Blessed Mother, and especially recalled her when in the presence of the Black Madonna. While he was growing up in Poland, Lolek often made pilgrimages to her shrine in Czestochowa.*

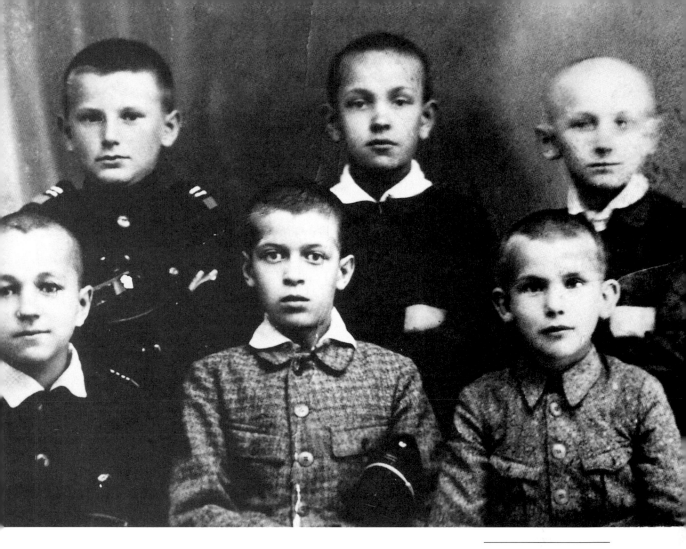

human heart. Karol Sr. lived a life of simple Christian humility. "Almost all of the memories of childhood are connected with my father," Lolek would write, years later, as pope. "His example alone was sufficient to inculcate discipline and a sense of duty." For Lolek, the most powerful image of childhood was that of his father down on his knees in prayer. This is precisely how, years later, the world would see John Paul II, whether he was kissing a tarmac on foreign soil or deep in prayer on the throne of St. Peter's.

Childhood for Lolek had its order and devotion, but it had its pleasures as well. While he could never escape the emotional cloud of his mother's suffering, his daily existence could hardly be called miserable. He had friends all over town, neighbors who looked in on him, and the aid of his parish. He knew how to play and when it came to his

PUBLIC SCHOOL: *Lolek attended an overcrowded public school in Wadowice but received a superb classical education. He was a straight-A student with a reputation as a hard and fast worker. In public school he made close friends with numerous Jews, many of whom were killed by the Nazis just a few years after this photograph was taken. He is seen here, in a uniform, top row, far left.*

favorite sports—soccer, ice skating, swimming, and skiing—Lolek was simply unstoppable. In all, his childhood was happy.

Then, when Lolek was eight, his mother died of heart and kidney failure. She was forty-five years old.

LIFE WITHOUT MOTHER

For a long time the family had known that Emilia was seriously ill, but even to those who knew him, Lolek seemed to handle her death with unusual strength. He did not wear his grief on his sleeve, crying openly only after his mother's funeral. (One of his teachers, stunned at the boy's fortitude, recalled him uttering that it was "God's will.") At home, however, he grieved and for months the atmosphere at 7 Church Street was an excruciating mix of Lolek's broken heart and his father's Polish stoicism.

With time, the grief of father and son was eased and the two found their way into an acceptable, even pleasurable rhythm of daily life. Karol Sr. would make breakfast and dinner, and the two would meet for lunch at a neighborhood place called Banas's restaurant. Money was scarce and Lolek was growing fast, so to outfit him, Karol Sr. would rip apart his old Army uniforms and remake them into shirts and pants for the boy. They moved Lolek's bed into the master bedroom, and the two shared the room. The parlor, which had fallen into disuse since Emilia's death, became a place to play indoor soccer, one-on-one. At night, father and son took long walks. Home was now strictly a male habitat, which was how Lolek would choose to live for the rest of his life.

By 1930 another factor lightened life in the Wojtyla household: Lolek's older brother, Edmund, graduated from medical school and moved closer to Wadowice to work as a physician at Bielsko-Biala hospital. Edmund often stayed with the family on weekends, and took his responsibility as Lolek's big brother quite seriously. Lolek idolized his older brother and relished the fact that Edmund was happy to spend time with him, romping around town and going to soccer matches. Time and circumstance, for the first time in their lives, had brought them together.

Catholicism, too, began to play an even greater role in the Wojtylas' reconstructed lives. Since Emilia's death, Lolek had become more and more devoted to his heavenly Mother, Mary, and father and son began the practice of daily Mass. Still, the young Lolek was not markedly pious; he didn't strike his friends as terribly preoccupied with God or the Church. Lolek was an altar boy, but so were many of his friends. He prayed often, but so did a lot of people. Had he not become pope, his childhood friends might simply have recalled him as a boy whose mother died. Conscientious. Intelligent. And a pretty good goalie.

Looking at the map, Wadowice is barely a dot. When Lolek was born, his hometown had a population of about eight thousand people. By the time he reached high school, only six families owned automobiles. Yet culturally and intellectually, Wadowice was quite sophisticated. The tiny metropolis had a reputation for outstanding classical education in the girls' and boys' public high schools. It also had a number of churches, two convents, two monasteries, three public libraries, and two amateur theaters. Regional theater is popular in Poland, and Wadowice, during Lolek's lifetime (in part because of Lolek) became nationally known for its exceptional productions.

It was into this gentrified community that Lolek emerged from his identity as a motherless child into a likable streetwise youngster who knew his way around town. At an early age he read and enjoyed poetry and often, to the disbelief of his friends, would attend esoteric theater productions. Languages came as easily to him as they had to his father, and he mastered Greek and Latin as a child.

Wadowice was not only a unique cultural center but, for Poland, it had an unusually peaceable mixture of Catholics and Jews. For centuries anti-Semitism

OVER THIS YOUR WHITE GRAVE

Over this your white grave
the flowers of life in white—
so many years without you—
how many have passed out of sight?

Over this your white grave
Covered for years, there is a stir
In the air, something uplifting
And, like death, beyond comprehension.

Over this your white grave
Oh, mother, can such loving cease?
For all his filial adoration
A prayer:
Give her eternal peace—

KAROL WOJTYLA
KRAKOW, SPRING 1939

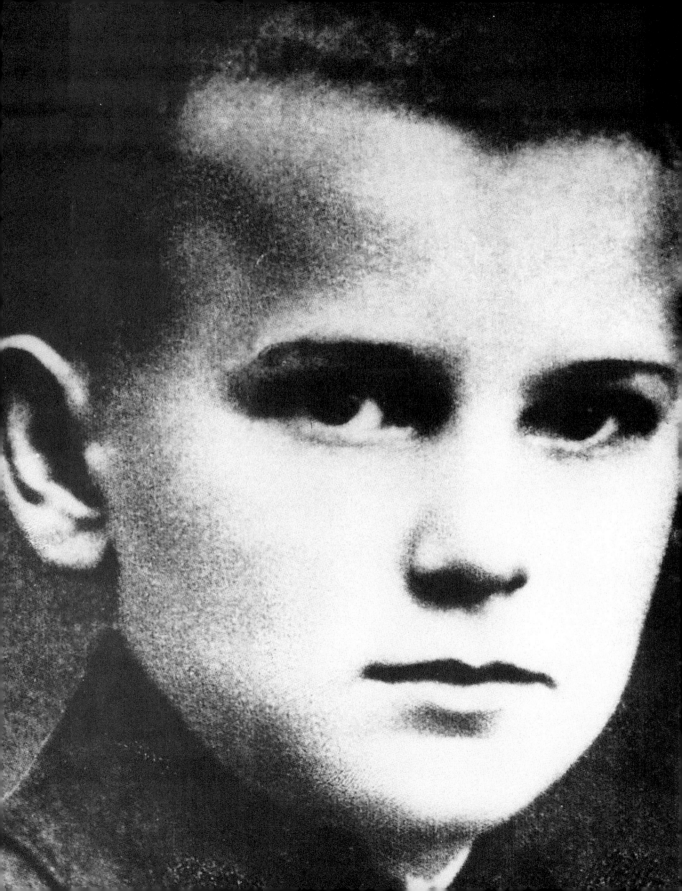

had raged in Poland but in the close-knit intellectual Wadowice, where roughly three-fourths of the people were Catholic and one-fourth were Jews, there was relatively little trouble.

Lolek was strongly influenced by Father Leonard Prochownik, the Wadowice parish priest who had officiated at his mother's funeral. Father Prochownik preached that anti-Semitism was "unchristian." It is difficult, perhaps, to conceive how radical a message that might have been, but for centuries Christian Poles had been overtly hostile to their Jewish neighbors, and there was ill-will on both sides.

For Lolek, anti-Semitism didn't resonate. His family rented their apartment from a Jewish family, and his neighbors were all Jewish. As a child Lolek attended public school, where many of his friends were Jewish. His school soccer team, which was primarily Jewish, played against the Catholic school team, and he was often asked to serve as goalie. One of his earliest childhood playmates, Jerzy Kluger, with whom he maintained a lifelong friendship, was Jewish. In modern circumstances this might not seem noteworthy, but for a Catholic Pole in his day and age, Lolek's relationship with Jews was quite unusual. As he grew older he would see anti-Semitism as an evil to be expunged from his Church. As pope, he would consider it one of his trademark issues.

It is impossible to speculate who Lolek might have become had he not had the benefit of the friends and the cultural influences of Wadowice. But it is fair to say that the future pope was as much raised by the people of Wadowice as by his father. Both father and son experienced a profound loneliness. Unlike his father, however, Lolek was not content to live in isolation. He was an avid outdoorsman and an athlete, and he could count every classmate as a friend. He loved poetry and philosophy, and he also had a great passion: the world of theater.

Across the street from Lolek's school lived Mieczyslaw Kotlarczyk and his family. Catholic and deeply intellectual, they were a second-generation theater family in Wadowice. Mieczyslaw was passionate about

TURNING INWARD: *By age twelve Lolek had lost his mother and his brother, Edmund. His brother's death from scarlet fever was sudden and crushing. At the time of this photograph, Lolek was beginning to move closer to God and his prayer life began to grow. His friends recall that he never seemed overly pious and didn't proselytize, but often lingered when passing before the Blessed Sacrament. In prayer, they recall, he would often lose his sense of time and place.*

MAN OF EMOTION

You don't really suffer when love is flooding you:
it's a patch of enthusiasm, pleasant and shallow;
if it dries up—do you think of the void?
Between heart and heart there is always a gap.
You must enter it slowly—
till the eye absorbs color,
the ear tunes to rhythm.

Love and move inward, discover your will,
shed heart's evasions and mind's harsh control.

—KAROL WOJTYLA

Mother Poland. Like so many Polish romantics, he viewed Poland as a redemptive nation, whose Christ-like suffering would bear fruits for Europe and the world. The Kotlarczyks were not well off, but their small home served as a salon for actors and actresses, and their amateur production company, Theater Circle, was highly respected. Mama Kotlarczyk loved Lolek, and he responded eagerly to her attentions and the camaraderie of sharing home-cooked food, laughter, and intense discussion. Lolek began spending more and more time with the family, helping out with stage sets and learning theater from behind the scenes. Soon he was visiting the Kotlarczyks after school every day. It isn't clear whether "The Lieutenant" was enthusiastic about Lolek's new friends. He apparently never spoke to them, choosing to wait in the street for Lolek in the late afternoon to walk him home. And though he obviously didn't discourage Lolek from acting, he also didn't encourage it. No one recalls ever seeing Karol Sr. at any of Lolek's dramatic performances.

Four years had passed since his mother died, and Lolek had not only reconstructed his life, he had established himself as a highly gifted, original character. He was all of twelve years old, and in many ways life could not have been better. So in 1932, when his brother Edmund suddenly died from a case of scarlet fever at the age of twenty-six, he was devastated. Whatever emotional balance Lolek had regained was completely overturned. Years later, in his book *Be Not Afraid,* written with French journalist André Frossard, the pope would recall with uncharacteristic emotion, "My mother's death made a deep impression . . . and my brother's perhaps a still deeper one because of the dramatic circumstances in which it occurred and because I was more mature. Thus quite soon I became a motherless only child."

It was a somber time. Father and son were once again on their own. In the months that followed, classmates observed Lolek spending more time in church, finding solace only in prayer. He still served as altar boy, but now instead of a single Mass, he was serving numerous Masses each day. He was an active member in Marian Sodality, a group that was devoted to the Virgin Mary. While his friends were rebelling in typically adolescent ways, Lolek was becoming quietly centered.

Friends, teachers, and neighbors weren't surprised; most of them figured it was a passing phase. After all, Lolek was not the first to turn

HALINA KWIATKOWSKA

Invariably, people wonder if Karol Wojtyla had a romantic interest before he became a priest. In Wadowice he was often associated with an actress named Halina Kwiatkowska, who was, according to those who knew her, gorgeous. Karol and Halina were often paired as the male and female romantic leads; they had key roles in the high school production of *Antigone,* starred in numerous local and regional productions, and then later in the highly esteemed underground theater in Krakow. Her father was the headmaster at the boys public high school, where Wojtyla was the top student in his class of about forty. The two *were* friends, but if anything, rather than romantically involved, they were competitive with each other. (She beat him in a major dramatic reading competition, and when Halina saw Wojtyla some fifty years later at Mass on the altar of St. Peter's, the first thing he said to her was: "You beat me!") They both loved theater and were probably the most serious and gifted in their dramatic circle; both of them had professional ambi-tions. They did dance together at the high school prom but Halina insists they were just close friends, and other former high school friends agree—though he had lots of friends who were female, Karol never had a real girlfriend.

Karol and Halina remained close for years. They both attended Jagiellonian University in Krakow until Hitler invaded Poland. During World War II, Halina courageously carried secret messages between friends, the Kotlarczyks in Wadowice and Karol in Krakow. She also performed with Karol in under-ground theater productions during the Nazi occupa-tion. Like Karol, she literally risked her life for the sake of art.

In 1946, when Karol Wojtyla became a priest, he performed his first baptism on Halina's first child, Monika Katarzyna.

Halina pursued her career and became nationally known in theater and television. To this day, she and Wojtyla correspond.

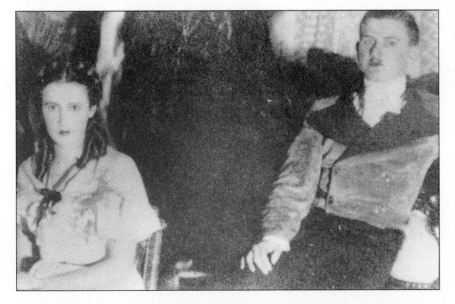

CHILDHOOD FRIENDS: *Halina Kwiatkowska is pictured in this faded photograph with young Karol Wojtyla. The two performed in local and regional theater throughout their youth in Wadowice, and later performed together in underground theater in Krakow, where they risked their lives to perform romantic and patriotic Polish plays in defiance of the Nazis.*

to God for consolation in a dark hour. But what Lolek was looking for in the wake of Edmund's death was not about passing phases. The reality of impermanence already had broken his heart.

EUROPE CLOSES IN

While twelve-year-old Lolek was turning inward to find peace, the world around him was becoming more agitated. In Europe, especially, Hitler and Stalin were gaining the upper hand.

Geographically and politically Poland was doomed. In 1932 Hitler had duped Britain and France into letting him take over neighboring Czechoslovakia. Hungary was a military state. Fascism was building in Italy. The Catholic Church, intent on combating Communism and Socialism, made pacts with the Fascists, who were not yet a menacing force.

In 1935, anti-Semitic attitudes throughout Europe began spilling into Poland, a country that was already hospitable to intolerance. Lolek was not a naïve person, but he was unprepared for the level of anti-Semitism he would witness in the coming years. Out-of-town gangs came into Wadowice to taunt Jews and picket their shops and businesses. Jerzy Kluger, Lolek's dear friend, recalled that Lolek would try to reason with people and make the case that "anti-Semitism was unchristian," but one guesses he was largely ignored. Like many Europeans, he might also have been in a state of denial or dangerous innocence. At one point, not grasping the underlying agenda, he accepted a theatrical role in a play about some Jewish socialists who were feigning to be Christians.

For Lolek, the seriousness of the situation became clear when his neighbor and friend Ginka Beer, who was then an actress, announced that she was moving to Palestine. Apparently she had been harassed at the University of Krakow, where she had been attending school. Karol Sr. was as devastated as Lolek, and tried to persuade her to stay: "Not all Poles are anti-Semitic. You know I am not!" he protested. Fortunately,

ST. STANISLAW: *Every schoolchild grew up learning about St. Stanislaw, the patron saint of Poland. Stanislaw, portrayed in the center image, was an eleventh-century bishop from Krakow who defied a despotic king and was martyred. Lolek revered St. Stanislaw from an early age and starred in a dramatization of his life during the war years. "All of life assumes a large number of tests of faith and character," Wojtyla would later write. "Saint Stanislaw is the patron of these tests."*

her intuitions were strong and she could not be swayed. Had she waited, she might have found her name on the transport list for Auschwitz.

In March 1938 German troops moved in to occupy Austria, but most Poles seemed unaffected and went about their day-to-day lives in a sort of oblivion.

Lolek continued to perform well in high school, where he was first in his class. By now he spoke Latin and Greek fluently, and in 1938 when the archbishop of Krakow, Prince Adam Stefan Sapieha, came to speak at commencement exercises, Lolek was given the honor of extending the school's formal welcome. The archbishop was not only a power in the Polish church, he was also an aristocrat and his bearing might have thrown off a less poised student. Apparently Lolek was so impressive that the archbishop asked school officials if there was a chance he intended to become a priest. At the time Lolek considered

WAWEL CATHEDRAL:
When Lolek came to Krakow, he and his father were filled with great expectation. The ancient city, once the royal capital of Poland and now its cultural center, was both medieval and modern, traditional and iconoclastic, in many ways a reflection of Lolek's worldview. He often went to Mass at Wawel Cathedral.

such a vocation unthinkable; he loved theater and aspired to study linguistics at the university. The archbishop was so informed. "What a shame," he is said to have remarked.

Despite Lolek's protestations, many of his high school friends saw signs that he had a vocation to the priesthood. They noticed that Lolek not only prayed when the church obliged him to but often in the middle of his day, in between homework assignments, or at random moments when most teenagers would be socializing. In the complex social hierarchy of high school, one might suspect that the academically gifted and prayerful Lolek might be regarded an outsider but he was actually immensely popular. Although he was considered one of the "group," many of his classmates refrained from using vulgar language around him. And while he had numerous friends who were female and he seemed very much at ease with girls, he never had a genuine girlfriend. While all of these behaviors might have added up to "future priest," Lolek shrugged off the idea. He was devoted to God, but he was an intellectual and was passionate about theater. He intended to serve God, but not as a man of the cloth.

Lolek had always planned on attending Jagiellonian University in Krakow. Following graduation from Wadowice High School in May 1938, he enlisted in a labor battalion for the military, a service required of all Poles his age. He fulfilled his obligation by spending approximately two weeks on a road construction crew. Once that work was complete, Lolek and his father packed their few things and vacated their rented flat at 7 Church Street.

TO KRAKOW

The journey from Wadowice to Krakow is just thirty miles, but the two cities are worlds apart. Krakow is the ancient royal capital of Poland, and the country's intellectual center. For Lolek, it must have seemed like moving to Oz.

As it happened, the Wojtylas had family in Krakow. Lolek's uncle on the maternal side, Robert Kaczorowski, owned a handsome slate-colored two-story house at 10 Tyniecka Street, where he lived with two of his unmarried sisters. He generously offered the Wojtylas a place to live. The Kaczorowskis lived on the first two floors, and the Wojtylas lived in the small dark basement, renting it for just a pittance. As close as the two families were physically, it appears that they had little or no contact during the six years they were together, perhaps a holdover from Emilia's father's decades-old disapproval of the marriage. However awkward the arrangement might have been, it was apparently the Kaczorowskis' generosity that made the move possible.

Moving to Krakow and bearing the cost of university life was going to be a virtual impossibility on Karol's small military pension, yet Karol and Lolek must have entered the royal city with great expectations. Lolek's expansive mind and theatrical talent had outgrown Wadowice. Founded in 1386, Jagiellonian University was the most highly respected scholarly institution in Poland and was a perfect fit for Lolek: intellectual and progressive, it operated at the highest academic standards. By this time he even looked the part. He was no longer the scrub-faced schoolboy in uniform, but a sort of bohemian. His hair was longish and he didn't wear a necktie. His clothes were what Poles then called "the poetic look."

Sixty-year-old Karol Sr. was weakened by an unspecified condition; still, the move to Krakow was not terribly burdensome. He had lived there before and knew the city well. In all probability, he didn't have much choice. He wasn't in good health, and the two could only afford living expenses if they lived together. Father and son set up their household and began the happy business of creating Lolek's academic plan, as if no real obstacles existed.

The future pope lost no time adjusting to Krakow. Within a month he knew his way around the city and the fast-paced university atmosphere. His first-year course list was onerous: Etymology of Polish Language, Polish Phonetics, First-Year Russian, Fourteenth- to Fifteenth-Century Polish Literature, Eighteenth-Century Polish Drama, Analysis of Drama Theory, The Work of Stanislaw Brzozowski, Dramatic Interpretation of Stanislaw Wyspianski, Contemporary Lyricism, History and Geography of Poland, and Introduction to Russian Literature, among others. He joined a dramatic troupe, some literary circles, and the sodality society devoted to the Blessed Virgin. On First Fridays he would attend mass at the Wawel Cathedral, seat of the archbishop of Krakow, and go to confession with Father Kazimierz Figlewicz, whom Lolek had known in Wadowice when the priest was vicar of Our Lady of Perpetual Help and a catechist at Lolek's high school.

Though Lolek is remembered as exceedingly private, he was by no means antisocial. In Krakow he made a large number of friends quickly. His classmates regarded him as a chaste character, certainly not one to socialize in bars or go to parties. (When things were about to

BLITZKRIEG: *In September 1939, soon after Lolek had settled in Krakow, the Nazis invaded. Poland was virtually defenseless against Hitler's phalanx of tanks and aircraft. This 1939 photo shows a German motorized attachment riding through a Polish town that was badly damaged by bombings by the Luftwaffe. When the invasion began, Lolek was assisting a priest during Mass at Wawel Cathedral.*

PRINCE ADAM SAPIEHA,
THE ARCHBISHOP OF KRAKOW

Karol Wojtyla met seventy-one-year-old Archbishop Sapieha as a high school student in Wadowice, where as the number one student in his class he was given the honor of greeting the esteemed archbishop. Karol and his classmates were not the only people who were impressed that day. Karol made a big impression on the archbishop, who was disappointed to learn that Karol was not interested in becoming a priest. The two met in Krakow four years later, when Karol decided to become one of Sapieha's secret seminarians.

Sapieha was an intriguing character. He was an elegant man, a titled prince, who came from a long line of Polish and Italian aristocrats, but he did not necessarily favor the bourgeois establishment of his day. He was independent, and willing to take enormous risks for what he believed in. During the Nazi occupation he established a secret seminary. Had his clandestine operation been discovered, he surely would have been imprisoned, or executed. Even more daring, Sapieha spoke out against anti-Semitism in the 1930s, and during the war aided Jews with papers, places to hide, and escape routes.

In 1945, with the Soviet encroachment, Sapieha had the prescience to create a newspaper so that the Church and the people would have a vehicle for communication. The newspaper, called *Tygodnik Powszechny* (Universal Weekly), was designed as a cultural medium and did not aim to discuss religion

PRINCE ADAM SAPIEHA: *The aristocrat Archbishop Sapieha met Wojtyla briefly when the future pope was in high school, and even then recognized that the young boy was exceptional. Later, when Wojtyla realized he had a calling to the priesthood, he asked to study in Sapieha's secret seminary in Krakow. Sapieha became a father figure to Wojtyla, and the two remained close until the archbishop's death.*

exclusively. Karol Wojtyla would be a frequent contributor. The first issue of *Tygodnik Powszechny* was published under the leadership of Father Jan Piwowarczyk, who hired Jerzy Turowicz as his deputy. Turowicz eventually was named editor-in-chief and served in that post into the 1990s. He became one of Karol Wojtyla's closest friends.

Sapieha was a tremendous influence in Karol Wojtyla's life, and carefully plotted out the young priest's career. After World War II ended he sent Wojtyla to Rome to pursue a more vigorous academic program than he had been able to offer in the Polish underground, and also insisted that Wojtyla tour all of Western Europe. When Wojtyla completed his doctoral work in Rome, Sapieha then sent him to the unlikely village of Niegowici to serve as priest to a largely uneducated, simple parish. After a few months he brought Wojtyla back to the culturally sophisticated Krakow and gave him a parish of intellectuals and bohemians. Once Wojtyla established himself as a pastoral success in Krakow, Sapieha abruptly directed him to return to scholarly work and pursue another doctorate, this time in philosophy.

In hindsight, there was a careful method to Sapieha's spiritual direction. In a few short years Wojtyla obtained two doctorates, worked with peasants and sophisticates, and toured all of Europe. Sapieha, in a sense, was John Paul's Merlin.

He died in 1951, at the age of eighty-four.

get rowdy, Lolek often began to "feel ill" and would excuse himself.) But none of Lolek's friends ever felt that he was disapproving or judgmental. He had piercing blue-gray eyes, an easy smile, and a dazzling curiosity. His passions were cerebral and romantic. He was often surrounded by his friends, but there was always a remoteness, a loneliness perhaps.

By 1939 Lolek had joined a theater group in Krakow called Studio 39. That summer they produced *Moon Cavalier.* He made numerous friendships within this group, especially with a student named Juliusz Kydrynski. Juliusz was literate, passionate about theater, and a devout Catholic. Overnight he became Lolek's best friend. In much the same way as the Kotlarczyks of Wadowice, the Kydrynski family adopted Lolek, and he began to share family dinners and lively conversations with them. Mrs. Kydrynski, a widow, doted on Lolek, and before long he referred to her as Mama. The household also included Juliusz's sis-

SOVIETS EVERYWHERE: *Soviet tanks rumble into a Polish town in August 1944. Karol Wojtyla's Poland was devastated by the Germans and Soviets in a matter of months.*

NAZIS ROUND UP JEWS AND POLES: *After the Nazi invasion in 1939, the Germans gathered up Jews and Poles to serve in labor camps and at Nazi-approved factories, where Karol Wojtyla was forced to work for several years. This photo, which was approved by Nazi censors in 1939, bizarrely shows the prisoners with slight smiles on their faces, no doubt on orders from their captors. The Nazis were intent on wiping out Jews, Polish intellectuals, and Polish Catholic clergy; the future pope fit directly into the second and third categories.*

ters, and Jadwiga Lewaj, a former French teacher, who boarded with the family. In Mrs. Lewaj, Lolek found yet another mother figure. He began to study French with her, eventually mastering the language through her tutorials.

Like the rest of Europe, Lolek seemed not to absorb the breadth and scope of Poland's political and military vulnerability—and the mounting consolidation of the Axis powers. Even news reports somehow did not penetrate. Germany had made territorial demands on Poland, which Poland had refused. Mussolini had made a pact with Hitler, and Hitler signed a treaty with Stalin, calling for the two powers to divvy up the land between them, which happened to be Poland.

On September 1, 1939, as was his practice, Lolek went to the four-teenth-century Wawel Cathedral for Mass and his First Friday confession with Father Figlewicz. On this particular morning, their voices echoed in the enormous church; there had been a civil defense warning and they were the only two people at Mass. While Karol helped Father serve at the altar, the church began to tremble. Planes swooped down, opening fire. The Nazis had begun their air attack on Krakow.

Father Figlewicz and Lolek finished celebrating the Mass, and Lolek left to check on his friends the Kydrynskis. Juliusz Kydrynski recalled that amid all of panic, Lolek moved easily and calmly. His steadiness was so powerful that it calmed others, even as the streets erupted into mayhem and fighter planes darkened the skies. Hitler had ordered three-fourths of his army into Poland in his first *blitzkrieg*. While the Poles ran to protect their loved ones and gather their things, some 2,500 German tanks began to rumble into their country. (The tanks would be met by the brave but futile attempts of the Polish cavalry, armed with sabers and lances.)

The Germans launched their attack from the west. Unaware · that Russia planned to invade from the east, the stupefied citizens of Krakow marched eastward on foot, carrying what they could on their backs. It was a pitiable parade of humans, farm animals, and carts. Once Lolek had helped the Kydrynskis, he rushed to his father, and they decided to join the evacuation. Karol Sr. was weak, but with the help of an occasional Polish army convoy, father and son made the trek about a hundred miles east of Krakow, where they believed they would be safe. When they arrived, they were greeted by the first wave of the Red Army. Overwhelmed,

(IN MEMORY OF A FELLOW WORKER)

1. He wasn't alone. His muscles grew into the flesh of the crowd,
energy their pulse, as long as they held a hammer,
as long as his feet felt the ground.
And a stone smashed his temples
and cut through his heart's chamber.

2. They took his body, and walked in a silent line.

3. Toil still lingered about him, a sense of wrong.
They wore gray blouses, boots ankle-deep in mud.
In this they showed the end.

4. How violently this time halted: the pointers on the low-voltage dials
jerked, then dropped to zero again.
White stone now within him, eating into his being,
taking over enough of him to turn him into stone.

5. Who will lift up that stone, unfurl his thoughts again
under the cracked temples? So plaster cracks on the wall.
They laid him down, his back on a sheet of gravel.
His wife came, worn out with worry; his son returned from school.

6. Should his anger now flow into the anger of others?
It was maturing in him through its own truth and love.
Should he be used by those who come after,
deprived of substance, unique and deeply his own?

7. The stones on the move again: a wagon bruising the flowers.
Again the electric current cuts deep into the walls.
But the man has taken with him the world's inner structure,
where the greater the anger, the higher the explosion of love.

—KAROL WOJTYLA, 1956

Karol Sr. and Lolek turned around and walked the hundred miles back to their basement apartment on Tyniecka Street, and waited.

With very little resistance, Krakow succumbed. The Polish government in Warsaw escaped to London and set up provisional headquarters. The primate of Poland, Cardinal August Hlond, went to Rome to report on the criminal acts of German aggression. He asked for the Pope's intervention. When he tried to return to Poland, the Germans blocked his way.

The Germans and the Russians divided up Poland into east and west zones, with a center zone called "General Government," where in fact Krakow was situated. Wadowice became part of Germany, as would a nearby Polish town called Oswiecim, or, in German, Auschwitz.

Honoring its mutual defense treaty with Poland, Britain declared war. But the invasion was a fait accompli. The Second World War had begun, but until the German invasion of France, it was a war of words.

POLAND: THE OCCUPATION

If the Poles had ignored signs of a German invasion, they were also slow to grasp what the Nazis meant to accomplish. The Germans did not just intend to occupy Poland, or even to exploit it. They meant to destroy it completely. They began this process in the first year of occupation by moving 1.2 million native Poles and 300,000 Jews from the German territories to the General Government zone. (If all of the Poles and Jews were in a single geographic location, their destruction could be carried out much more efficiently.) The Russians had a similar objective: within two years, 1.5 million Poles had been shipped from the Russian zone to Siberian camps. Most of them were never heard from again.

According to the Nazi plan, every vestige of Polish culture and nationality was to be erased from the state's consciousness. The first

wave of assault would be against the
Catholic clergy, the Jewish leaders, the
nobility, and the intellectuals, since these
groups were considered the most influential. Once the "the elite" was eradicated,
the Nazis planned to make the citizenry
of Warsaw into slaves to produce supplies
for the Germans. Eventually they
intended to purge Krakow of all its
250,000 Polish residents and rebuild the
city as an idealized German metropolis.
To accomplish Hitler's goals, the General
Government was put under the direction
of the formidable Nazi Governor-
General Hans Frank.

Wawel Cathedral was closed,
although the Nazis later allowed Mass to
be celebrated two times a week, in an empty church under military
guard. Polish art collections were seized, including masterpieces from
Polish churches and museums. Jagiellonian University was shut down.
The Krakow seminary was boarded up and turned into barracks for
the occupying forces. Ordinations were banned. Monks, nuns, and
priests throughout the German zone of Poland were sent to concentration camps, where, ultimately, thousands of them were killed.

And while the Nazis were weeding out all of Poland's religious, intellectual, and political leaders, they also were drafting every able-bodied Pole
to their cause. All Poles (including most women) were required to obtain
an *Ausweiss* identity card. The card was granted only to employees of
German-approved work; basically that meant war materials. If you were
caught without a card, you were shipped to forced labor camps, or shot.

Karol Sr. was now more than sixty years old, and the Germans had
cut off his military pension. Desperate for money and some kind of
employment, Lolek took a job as a restaurant delivery boy. But the
delivery job, which could hardly be described as part of the war effort,
placed Lolek at an enormous risk. Roundups were occurring at all
hours, and catching Lolek—sturdy, young, and an intellectual—would
have been a bonus for the Germans.

THE SOVIETS INVADE:
*Soon after the Nazis
launched their invasion from
the west, the Soviets entered
Poland from the east, seizing
their "share" in the partition
agreed upon by Germany
and Russia. This photo,
approved by censors, shows a
pair of Soviet officers
attempting to befriend a
Polish woman.*

SOVIET PROPAGANDA:
While the Germans ultimately intended to wipe out the Poles, the Soviets planned to dominate them. Thus when the Soviets invaded Poland, they attempted to develop a small measure of goodwill. This photo shows Soviet political workers distributing Russian newspapers in 1939 in Poland. The "Red Spellbinders," as they were called, attempted straightaway to get the Polish people interested in the Communist agenda.

In the fall of 1940, somewhat serendipitously, Lolek and a handful of his colleagues—including his best friend, Juliusz—found employment at a stone quarry at Zakrzowek, about three miles from Lolek's Tyniecka Street apartment. The quarry produced a compound used in making explosives, and though it previously had been privately owned, the Nazis now ran the operation. This meant that work at the quarry qualified for the coveted *Ausweiss* card. Lolek's task was to blast and heave limestone onto a rail car for export; he also worked on the tracks and sometimes maintained the rail lines. It was a brutal enterprise, but it was a job, and it would buy his relative safety even if it did not pay the rent.

Lolek's experience working in the quarry had an enormous effect on his social and political philosophy, and ultimately his papacy. For centuries, even in modern times, most papal candidates had been bred like royalty; their breeding included scholastic and clerical education but certainly not any activity that callused their hands. For four years, under Nazi supervision, Lolek worked long days as a menial laborer lifting huge rocks, with only one fifteen-minute break, during which time he was allowed a small meal of black bread and coffee and the heat of an iron stove. And it was cold; during the harsh Polish winters, the temperatures stayed well below zero.

While he was lifting boulders and mending rail lines, Lolek also was thinking. Over time, amid the pounding of mallets, he developed his own economic philosophy that would become a cornerstone of his papacy. Economically, his sympathies were left-leaning, but rather than seeing Marxism or Communism as the path to social and economic parity, Lolek saw a middle ground, which he would spend his life defining.

PATRIOTIC THEATER:
THE UNDERGROUND

When he was not working in the quarry, Lolek could often be found at the Kydrynskis, where he would enjoy "Mama's" attentions and work with Juliusz on various theater projects, generally assuming the role of director. The Germans had banned all Polish theater, but Lolek and his friends pursued their work, secretly rehearsing classical Polish plays, and occasionally even performing them in the Kydrynskis' living room apartment before a handful of invited guests, who literally risked their lives for the experience.

In the first years of the occupation, thousands of Polish intellectuals were haphazardly executed by the Germans, generally at the whim of the officer in charge. Soon the elimination of the Polish elite was a direct order from Nazi Germany. As the persecution intensified, it produced a backlash: the writers and artists and performers of Poland, especially Krakow, became even more animated, producing volumes of underground literature, art, and drama. Lolek pursued his theater life passionately. He also began to write poetry. Like so many in his literary generation, he was influenced greatly by Polish romanticists, messianics, and lyricists. Lolek was writing poetry constantly, almost obsessively, a habit that has continued all his life.

Under any circumstances Lolek's literary and theatrical output would be considered staggering—especially taking into account that eight hours of his day was devoted to hard labor at the quarry, along with a three-mile walk to work and back. Amazingly, during this period, he not only wrote poetry, but even composed three plays on biblical subjects.

Hitler figured he could negotiate with the Catholic Church in Italy through Mussolini, and with the German bishops in his own country. But he considered the Catholic Church in Poland too powerful, and

NARROW ESCAPES

Most people recall the assassination attempt on the Holy Father in 1981, when the Turkish gunman Mehmet Ali Agca attempted to kill him as he greeted the faithful in St. Peter's Square. But it was not the first time John Paul II eluded death.

When he was growing up in Wadowice, the future pope spent much of his social time at Banas's Restaurant, sort of a bar and coffee shop just downstairs from his apartment at 7 Church Street. When Wojtyla was about nine years old, one of the Banas children picked up a pistol that was lying on the counter, apparently left by a policeman who frequented the restaurant. It went off, missing Wojtyla by mere inches.

On another occasion, when Wojtyla was working in the chemical factory in occupied Krakow, he also was nearly killed. As it happened, Wojtyla had worked a double shift and was walking the five-mile course home late one evening when a German army truck bumped him off the road. Wojtyla's body flew into a ditch and for several hours he was left for

dead. A woman who lived on the street found the future pope in a coma. She went for help and the German officer she located ordered her to take Wojtyla to the hospital, where he spent three weeks in bed until another patient in more critical condition took his place.

On Black Sunday in Krakow, the Nazis went door to door, looking for every able-bodied Polish male in the city. In all they rounded up more than eight thousand Poles and deported them to concentration camps, where most of them died. When the Nazis knocked at the door of the house on Tyniecka Street and no one answered, they broke into the first and second floors. For some reason, they passed over the basement apartment, where Karol was on his knees, praying.

In 1982, a year to the day from the 1981 assassination attempt, the pope visited Fatima, Portugal, to thank the Blessed Mother for what he believed was her intercession in the thwarted attempt to kill him. Once again, a deranged individual tried to kill the pope. He was stopped in his attempt to lunge at the Holy Father with a knife.

therefore an institution to be destroyed. Polish priests were being relocated to concentration camps and executed daily.

To make up for the shortage of clergy, a network of lay people began to assume responsibility for the nonsacramental but vitally important community work. Youth groups, especially, needed supervision. In February 1940 Lolek attended a prayer group for youth called the Living Rosary at St. Stanislaw Kostka Church, and it was there that he met Jan Leopold Tyranowski, a man who would become a central character in his life.

Tyranowski was a strange bird, beginning with his appearance. He was a short man with long, silvery, unkempt hair and blue eyes that seemed to be fixed on something other than the physical world. He was trained as an accountant but had abandoned that profession to work in his family's business as a tailor. He liked sewing, he said, because it gave him more time to meditate and pray while he worked.

Not everyone liked Tyranowski, at least on first impression. Apparently he spoke in somewhat old-fashioned, off-putting language, and some people didn't like what they perceived as his all-or-nothing religious mentality. Mieczyslaw Malinski, who also met Lolek at the Living Rosary youth group (and who later also became a priest) described Tyranowski as heavy-handed, though genuinely filled with grace.

But Lolek found in Tyranowski a teacher as worthy of leading him to God as Kotlarcyzk was in leading him to art. Tyranowski might have been socially awkward and somewhat zealous, but Lolek saw beyond the rough edges and was deeply moved by Tyranowski's beliefs. His life had been profoundly influenced by St. John of the Cross and St. Teresa of Avila, Spanish mystics from the sixteenth century, and certainly Tyranowski was a mystic himself. Through the writings of St. John, especially, Tyranowski introduced Lolek to the practice of interior prayer. He served as Lolek's spiritual director, visiting with him privately to review his moral and spiritual encounters as they had unfolded during the week. Some evenings before sunset he would go to the Wojtylas' home and read Scripture. He even walked Lolek to the labor camp at the quarry from time to time, so they would have time together to pray and to reflect.

Tyranowski's primary contribution to the future pope's spiritual

SELLING COMMUNISM:
The Soviets expended great effort breaking down the resistance of the Polish people by "selling" them on the virtues of Communism. This would serve the Soviet agenda after the war ended, when they took over all of Poland.

life, as Lolek himself put it, was this: "He proved that one cannot only learn about God, but that one can live through God." It was, perhaps, the most transforming truth of Lolek's life.

Lolek believed that Tyranowski was "one of those unknown saints, hidden amid the others like a marvelous light at the bottom of life, at a depth where night usually reigns. He disclosed to me the riches of his inner life, of his mystical life. In his words, in his spirituality, and in the example of a life given to God alone, he represented a new world that I did not yet know. I saw the beauty of a soul opened up by grace."

Most people who knew the pope as a young man agree that without the providential intersection of Lolek and Tyranowski, the pope might never have become a priest. Yet even at that point, Lolek was not aware of his vocation.

THE FINAL LOSS

By the early winter of 1941, Karol Sr. was confined to bed. Lolek was in charge of housekeeping and bringing home dinner, usually a hot meal from the Kydrynskis' kitchen. That year Karol Sr. would celebrate his last Christmas. On February 18 Lolek and Juliusz's sister, Maria Kydrynski, brought some dinner to Karol Sr., along with some medicines they were able to obtain from a public health dispensary. When they arrived, they found Karol Sr. collapsed over his bed. He was dead at age sixty-two, apparently from a heart attack.

Lolek called for a priest. He was upset that he had not been present at his father's deathbed, just as he had been absent when his mother and brother died. His friend Juliusz rushed over, and they spent the whole night at the feet of Karol Sr.'s body. They talked about death and they prayed.

Karol Sr. was buried on February 22 at a military cemetery in Krakow. Father Figlewicz presided at the funeral. The future pope now felt truly alone. "At twenty," he later said, "I had already lost all the people I loved."

The Kydrynskis invited Lolek to live with them for a while, and he did, for six months. Every day after work, Lolek would go across town to the military cemetery and pray at Karol Sr.'s grave. He continued his practice of daily Mass, as he had since his mother's death. He continued to meet and to pray with Tyranowski.

The death of his father would serve as a change in course, gently directing Lolek . . . to the priesthood.

ROME

———∞∞∞———

1942 TO 1978

Visitabo oves meas, dicit Dominus, et
suscitabo pastorem qui pascat eas.

*(I will look after my sheep, says the Lord, and I
will raise up one shepherd who will pasture them.)*

—Ezekiel 34:11.23–24

THE SECRET SEMINARIAN

It had been two years since the Nazis invaded Poland, and life for Karol Wojtyla had changed in almost every respect. He was no longer the bohemian intellectual at the prestigious Jagiellonian University, but a common laborer at a chemical factory. The Germans had banned Polish literature and theater; even writing a poem was now against the law. His father was dead.

Only God hadn't changed. Karol still maintained his underground studies with Jan Tyranowski, his spiritual director, and his prayer life had become almost indistinguishable from his active life. He still went to monthly confession with Father Figlewicz on First Friday, though it now took place in secret at the priest's residence across from the Wawel Cathedral.

One fall afternoon in 1942, after working a day shift at the factory, Karol took along a friend, Mieczyslaw Malinski, to his monthly confession at the Wawel rectory. Karol and the priest retreated to a private setting, while Malinski sipped a cup of tea.

Malinski waited, lingering over his cup of tea as long as he could. The minutes ticked by, and he began to feel uneasy. An hour passed. What confession could take this long? Finally, to Malinski's relief, Karol and the priest emerged. Karol apologized to his friend for the delay, and the two headed out into the cool autumn night.

They walked silently for several blocks, and then Karol gave him the news: he had decided to become a priest.

On learning of Karol's decision that afternoon, while Malinski waited with his empty tea cup, Father Figlewicz had slipped Karol in to meet with Archbishop Sapieha. Karol had met the aristocratic, elegant bishop years before in Wadowice, when he extended the school's official greeting to Sapieha at commencement exercises. The archbishop remembered Karol well, and accepted him into his secret seminary at once.

There were risks involved. Already more than two dozen priests in Krakow had been rounded up and sent to concentration camps. The seminary was a secret for good reason: everyone who knew about it, let alone studied at it, was a candidate for the concentration camps or firing squad. But Karol had made his decision. Later, he would explain, "After my father's death, I gradually became aware of my true path. I was working at the factory and devoting myself, as far as the terrors of the occupation allowed, to my taste for literature and drama. My priestly vocation took place in the midst of all that, like an inner fact of absolute clarity. . . . In autumn [1942] I knew that I was called. I could see clearly what I had to give up, and the goal that I had to attain, without a backward glance."

With the exception of Malinski, no one in Karol's circle of friends and acquaintances knew he was studying to become a priest, not even his roommates. The Kotlarczyks, his beloved theater family, had moved from Wadowice to Krakow, and now shared his basement flat on Tyniecka Street. With Karol's help they had also formed an acclaimed underground theater group in Krakow called Rhapsodic Theater, and Karol starred in many of their productions. Though the Kotlarczyks lived and worked together with Karol in a cramped apartment, they remained unaware of his secret life for more than a year.

Obviously Karol had an enormous fund of energy. In the early hours of the morning he would go to church, walk across town to pray at his father's grave, and head to a factory job five miles in the other direction, where he put in a full shift. After work he would meet with his spiritual director, Jan Tyranowski, or with Archbishop Sapieha, then rehearse any number of plays with the Rhapsodic Theater. While Krakow slept, he took up his seminary work: reading religious texts, writing papers, and preparing for the archbishop's rigorous examinations.

Karol continued his acting with Rhapsodic Theater until 1943, when he finally told Kotlarczyk that he had been studying for the priesthood and that he would no longer be able to maintain his acting career. His mentor did not take the news well.

FENCES AT AUSCHWITZ: *Not too far from Wadowice, where the future pope spent his childhood, was a Polish town called Oswiecim. The Germans later renamed it Auschwitz, and it became a concentration camp of horrors. The heinous treatment of the Jews during World War II, many of them Lolek's dear friends, affected him deeply. Having been so close—both physically and emotionally— to the travesty of the Holocaust, it is not surprising that Wojtyla has been the most influential and powerful proponent of healing Christian and Jewish relations in the twentieth century.*

It was not a matter of Kotlarczyk not being religious—quite the contrary, he was a devout Catholic. But Karol's theatrical talents were considerable; he was regarded as one of the great actors in Krakow. As a moral and cultural propagandist, Kotlarczyk regarded Karol as a powerful instrument for the underground Polish liberation movement. Repeatedly Kotlarczyk and Karol's other acting friends begged him not to abandon the theater, waging an elaborate intellectual campaign that employed scripture, poets, and philosophers to make the case that he should not misappropriate the theatrical talents God had given him. But Karol gently rejected their arguments. He had not only made up his mind to quit acting, but in a sense he was prepared to quit the world. At that point he wanted to join a contemplative Carmelite order and live the life of a monk, choosing prayer as his means to liberate his motherland and his own soul.

As saddened as they were, no one in his circle could say in hindsight they were surprised; they had always known that Karol was deeply religious. But the loss of his prodigious talent and intelligent presence rocked Poland's classical theatrical world.

Withdrawing from the camaraderie and intense relationships of the theater company, Karol now entered a new and singular phase of life, focused solely on work at the factory and his theological studies. He no longer hid his vocation from his friends, but his new life remained hidden to the rest of the world. Under Archbishop Sapieha's direction, ten young men were studying for the priesthood in Krakow at the time. Each seminarian received his instruction in private and, for security reasons, none of them knew who else, if anyone, might be in training. Karol was required to read theological texts of extraordinary difficulty, even for his vast mind. (He complained that it took him all of two weeks to absorb one very complex book on metaphysics.) The spiritual works he was now reading lifted him into a new level of intellectual intoxication, and whenever he had a free moment at work he could be found reading some dense spiritual tome. Workers also remember him praying at the factory unabashedly, often on his knees.

During this period, Mieczyslaw Malinski, under the spiritual direction of Tyranowski, also decided to become a priest. Karol took him to the Wawel rectory, and Malinski made the same visit to Archbishop Sapieha, who accepted him too as a secret seminarian.

LONG DAYS: *Like other Poles, Wojtyla was forced by the Nazis to work in labor camps during the early 1940s. He first worked in a stone quarry, breaking rocks and loading rail cars. He later gained employment at the Solvay chemical plant. During this time, he was sleeping only a few hours a night: he worked in the chemical factory all day, spent his evenings at the underground Rhapsodic Theater (where he acted in and directed Polish patriotic plays), and devoted the early hours of the morning to prayer and his secret studies for the priesthood.*

CATHOLIC ECONOMICS

"Work . . . manifests man's resemblance to God."
—Pope John Paul II, Rome 1987

While working as a common laborer during the war, Wojtyla developed an appreciation of the sanctity of work. (This was later expressed in his devotion to *Opus Dei,* the lay movement dedicated to the sanctification of work, which eventually became a Personal Prelature.) He found dignity in his simple, arduous tasks, breaking stones in the quarry and working at the Solvay Chemical Plant. His enormous respect for work provoked him to study economic systems from the standpoint of the worker and, indeed, when he became a cardinal he was known as the Workers' Cardinal.

In his late twenties Father Wojtyla was able to visit with intellectuals throughout postwar Western Europe thanks to the largesse of Archbishop Sapieha, who wanted Wojtyla to understand the Church in its universal context, rather than as a provincial Pole. It was an intellectually vigorous period of reexamination. After World War II major Catholic philosophers, especially in France, were exploring economic systems and their relation to the dignity of the individual human being. Church fathers were intent on assessing these systems in relation to Christian justice. How did one balance freedom and fairness?

Humanity, Wojtyla had determined, now found itself in one of three categories: totalitarian systems, where people were enslaved; democratic, capitalistic systems, where people were corrupted by materialism, riches, and greed; and Third World systems, where people lived in poverty. He viscerally condemned the greed of capitalism and realized that while some of the ideals of communism and socialism sounded worthwhile, they too often devolved into totalitarian systems, clearly the worser evil. The Third World, with its dictators and tribal feuds, had only institutionalized economic poverty. The Catholic objective, and certainly Wojtyla's, was to determine which economic and political means respected the dignity of the human being, preserved freedom, protected and ennobled the worker, and granted opportunity—without encouraging materialism and greed.

Much of the Catholic debate about economics that began after World War II would fuel Wojtyla's personal crusades against not only the concept of Marxist autocracy, but capitalist exploitation as well. Over the course of his papacy Wojtyla would make it clear that it is not the Church's intent or purview to dictate economic policy, but that it would continue to serve as the world's conscience, when human rights were violated or human souls were corrupted. As pope, with his own moral authority, he would challenge the world's great economic systems, one at a time.

DEFENDING THE WORKER: *During his priesthood Wojtyla developed a deep respect for the common worker, believing work to be a fundamental source of dignity for humankind. He tirelessly advocated on behalf of workers. When the Soviets occupied Poland and kept wages low—and food prices high—he supported nonviolent means to achieve just economic ends, including peaceful strikes conducted by these shipyard workers from Gdansk.*

POLAND DOUBLE-CROSSED

By now Stalin had joined forces with the Allies and at the "Big Three" meeting in Tehran in 1943, Churchill, Stalin, and Roosevelt carved up Poland again, allocating much of the original Poland to Russia on the east and returning the German-occupied Poland back to Poland on the west. The provisional Polish government in London went along with this; mostly what they lost in the agreement was eastern territory occupied by Ukrainians and others who weren't actually Polish. What the world—including, disturbingly, Churchill and Roosevelt—didn't realize was that Stalin planned a double-cross; no matter what was agreed upon, he intended to take over the whole of Poland anyway.

And he wasted no time. Soon after the Big Three meeting, Stalin initiated his strategy to "liberate" the Poles from the Germans. Warsaw was first on the list. After guaranteeing massive military backup, Stalin stirred the Poles into a rebellion on July 31, 1944, letting them initiate the first bloody wave of combat against the Germans. With a mere four days of ammunition, the Poles rose up against their German oppressors in the famous Warsaw Uprising. They fought valiantly against the Nazi counterattack, trying to hold on until Russian reinforcements arrived. The Russians never came. Instead, the Russians held back and watched as Warsaw was leveled. Once the Poles were defeated, Stalin's troops marched in, knocked over the exhausted Germans, and took Warsaw.

On August 6—Black Sunday—the Germans, seeing the writing on the wall, turned their attention to Krakow, and as a preemptive measure arrested more than eight thousand men and boys, figuring they could at least deflect a Krakow uprising. The Germans went door to door, rousing the Polish males from their sleep or yanking them out of hiding. The raid reached Karol's house on Tyniecka Street. Rather than fleeing, Karol prayed, in terror. When the Nazis finally reached the house and banged on the door, there was no answer. They searched the first and second floors of the house but mysteriously passed by the basement apartment. Their search complete, they moved to the next house, looking for more Polish males, and leaving the future pope trembling in the basement.

The war in Poland had reached a new and dangerous pitch. Archbishop Sapieha decided that his secret seminarians needed sanctuary, so he sent trusted parishioners—housewives, laborers, physicians, journalists—all over the city to find his ten students and smuggle them into the archbishop's residence. By morning all the young men were safe within the palace walls, and a makeshift dormitory was put into place. Karol arrived in his torn working pants and wooden clogs; he brought some of his journals but no other belongings. Each of the young men was given a clerical robe to wear and assigned an iron bed in the large hall of the palace, where they would stay until the war was over.

It is remarkable how in a matter of months the Nazis had transformed all of occupied Poland into a prison. When Karol did not show up for work in the factory, his absence was immediately reported. His foreman told the authorities, and within hours Nazi officers came looking for him at the Tyniecka Street apartment. When they discovered he had disappeared, they interrogated his intellectual and theater friends. The Nazis' citywide search for Wojtyla became so intense that the archbishop was alerted; using his underground network of loyal Catholics, he somehow finessed a bureaucratic change in the factory's employment rolls, effectively calling off the manhunt. Whoever eliminated his name from the rolls—thus diffusing the Nazis' search—saved the life of Karol Wojtyla.

The secret seminarians stayed in hiding and read and studied and prayed, protected by the glass of ancient windows and the gates of the archbishop's palace, which in keeping with tradition was accorded the status of sanctuary. Just beyond, Germans marched in lockstep, innocent civilians were arrested, tanks passed through. There were also screams, and the occasional sound of gunfire. The young men who had joined the secret seminary to serve their fellow Poles were now hopelessly cut off from them.

Finally, the war ended. On January 17, 1945, the Germans left Krakow. The following day, the Soviets moved in.

Wishful thinkers, many Poles greeted them with open arms.

TOURING EUROPE: *After the war was over, Archbishop Sapieha directed young Father Wojtyla to leave Poland and go to Rome to study for his doctorate in theology. He wanted Wojtyla to broaden his horizons, and encouraged him to tour as much of Europe as he could. Clearly Sapieha, an aristocratic and sophisticated man, believed Wojtyla would be a major asset to the Polish Church.*

JEWISH QUARTERS: *In 1941 the Jewish district of Kazimierz became a walled ghetto. Over the course of the war, the Nazis killed most of Poland's Jews. This is what remains today: the sparsely populated Jewish quarter in modern Krakow.*

THE SOVIET TAKEOVER

During the war, while the prime minister of Poland set up a provisional government in London, the members of the Polish Communist party relocated to Russia. At the war's end, the Yalta Conference installed a "coalition" government in Poland, composed of these two parties, with the Communists very much in control and the anti- or non-Communists represented marginally. The Communists were poised for a complete takeover, and they wouldn't encounter much resistance. For a good number of Poles, Communism sounded almost reasonable, especially if one didn't read the fine print.

The Church in Poland did not embrace the new Soviet-controlled leadership, but it did not reject it either. For the next forty-five years, it would perform a careful dance with the Communists, offering a concession here or there to keep peace on the streets—and the church doors open. While the Polish Church had decided that its only hope was to keep the dance going, the Vatican had decided it would have nothing to do with the Communists, launching a major assault on Communism in its many forms all over the world. This complicated matters for the Poles, to say the least.

Archbishop Sapieha was clearly aligned with the Vatican on this matter, and found himself in conflict with the Polish bishops in the following decades. Not only did he have to deal with the Communists but he had to work with the political machinations of the Polish Church. One of the shrewdest moves he made early in the Communist takeover was to found a newspaper that would be instrumental in liberating Poland. Under the aegis of the Church, Sapieha created *Tygodnik Powszechny*—the "Universal Weekly" (catholic means "universal"). The name suggested that the newspaper was not just a religious publication, and in fact the paper covered almost every topic imaginable. Sapieha staffed the paper with Catholic professional journalists and provided office space and financial support. One of its regular contributors would be Karol Wojtyla, under his own name at first, and then under a variety of pseudonyms, depending on the subject.

With the war over, the secret seminarians were able to leave the archbishop's palace and pursue their vocations in full view. Karol worked to complete his studies and, having passed his theological exams, was ordained as a priest in Cardinal Sapieha's private chapel on November 1, 1946, the Feast of All Saints.

On November 2, the Feast of All Souls, Father Wojtyla performed his first Mass at Wawel Cathedral, dedicating his priestly works to his father, mother, and brother. All the members of the Rhapsodic Theater attended, along with Father Figlewicz. At Father Wojtyla's next Mass, which was celebrated

ST. THOMAS AQUINAS: *Father Wojtyla studied the works of St. Thomas Aquinas while he attended the Angelicum University in Rome under the tutleage of Father Garrigou-Lagrange, one of the leading theologians of his day. Wojtyla also studied the works of the mystic St. John of the Cross, who had a powerful influence in the future pope's prayer life.*

S. THOMAS AQVINAS.
Si sacra Christiadum liceat conferre profanis, Alcidem contra te faciam haereticos. Tu tollis, veluti Alcides vicisse tot hydras Creditur, antidotis dira venena tuis.

in his neighborhood church, Jan Tyranowski was among those present.

Thousands of Polish priests had been killed or maimed during the war, so most sacramental functions had been suppressed. With peace came a huge demand for baptisms, weddings, confessions, confirmations, and memorial Masses. Sapieha wasted no time in dispatching his secret seminarians throughout the diocese. But he made two exceptions. He decided that rather than serving in local parishes like most of the seminarians, Father Wojtyla and another student, Father Stanislaw Starowieyski, should continue their education, and obtain the equivalent of master's degrees in theology—in Rome. However rigorous Sapieha had tried to be with his secret seminarian project, he felt that these two students needed exposure to the world outside Poland, advanced degrees in theology, and a little experience with Roman politics.

On November 15, 1946, Fathers Wojtyla and Stanislaw boarded a train. Traveling third-class on a train crowded with refugees, they made their way to the Eternal City.

VIA ROMA

To a man with a classical education and a giant intellect and soul, Rome must have seemed a kind of homecoming. Yet in his letters home to Poland, Father Wojtyla never expressed an emotional reaction to the Eternal City. Actually, his Roman correspondence sounds rather flat; somewhere around the level of travelogue. But one surmises that this is not so much a measure of his feelings, but of his extraordinary reserve.

True, it was postwar Rome. The city was charred and confused, and the people weary. But it still was Rome. Fathers Wojtyla and Stanislaw were sent to study at the sixteenth-century Angelicum University, a Domincan-run institution. The two Poles were to reside at the Belgian College, which housed young priests and seminarians. The quarters were dreadful, and offered no plumbing or heat. Karol remembers trying to stay warm with "a hot plate under his chair."

PADRE PIO

One of the most beloved and controversial candidates for sainthood is Father Francesco Forgione, known as Padre Pio. He was a Capuchin monk who lived in a Mount Gargano village called San Giovanni Rotondo, near Foggia, Italy.

Padre Pio has many more admirers than detractors, and Father Wojtyla fell squarely into the former category. As early as 1947, at his first chance, Father Wojtyla made the journey to see Padre Pio, to make his confession.

Padre Pio was known for his mystical healings, his relationships with angels, his penetrating confessions, and the stigmata he experienced since the 1920s. He was often in the center of spiritual warfare, and recorded many instances of having to fend off demons with Christ's help.

Until John Paul II, the Church's response to Padre Pio had ranged from standoffish to closing him down. Wojtyla has never refuted or commented on the story that in his 1947 visit to Padre Pio, the monk was somewhat startled when Wojtyla approached. It is said that Padre Pio knelt at Wojtyla's feet, and prophesied that in time Wojtyla would be pope. He also foresaw that Wojtyla would be the victim of an assassination attempt. At the time of this encounter, Padre Pio was somewhat of an outcast. But Wojtyla found him to be a holy man, and believed deeply in his proximity to God.

Wojtyla turned to Padre Pio in 1962 when his dear friend Dr. Wanda Poltawska was diagnosed with colon cancer, and asked that Padre Pio pray for her recovery. Surgery had been recommended but apparently her prognosis was not good. After Padre Pio received the letter, she did go into instantaneous remission, and the record of that transaction was part of the documentation in the files proposing his beatification, which was held in Rome on May 2, 1999.

PRIMATE CARDINAL WYSZYNSKI: *Cardinal Wyszynski was an important figure in Karol Wojtyla's life and in the history of postwar Poland. The future pope collaborated with the cardinal on many religious and political efforts to free the Poles. Wyszynski spearheaded the momentous Great Novena, celebrating one thousand years of Christianity in Poland—and also dealing the Communists a serious symbolic blow.*

As lacking as the accommodations were, the academics were superior. Father Wojtyla quickly found a mentor at the university, a professor named Father Réginald Garrigou-Lagrange, one of the most respected theologians of his time. Father Garrigou-Lagrange took a personal interest in Wojtyla, no doubt delighted that his two areas of particular expertise—St. Thomas Aquinas and St. John of the Cross—were also the subjects about which Wojtyla was most passionate. St. Thomas Aquinas was a master logician and rationalist, while St. John of the Cross was a mystic. Though the saints did not in any sense contradict each other, only an intellect of St. Thomas's capacity might conceive of a paradigm where rationalism and mysticism operated in harmony. Wojtyla would not only grasp the paradigm—but live it.

Father Wojtyla escaped from his studies long enough to take several trips around Italy, touring all of its great shrines and churches and cathedrals. He went to Assisi, Florence, Siena, Milan, and Venice. He also sought out a Capuchin monk called Padre Pio at San Giovanni Rotondo in a village near Foggia in Apulia, Italy.

On July 15, 1947, Jan Tyranowski died after a long and painful illness. Father Wojtyla had tried repeatedly to get permission to be with him but, for reasons unknown, Sapieha refused his requests, insisting that he continue his European travels and return to Rome to complete his postgraduate work. It must have been a difficult lesson in obedience, but Father Wojtyla deferred with grace. He returned to Rome and completed his 280-page dissertation, written in Latin, and entitled "The Virtue of Faith in St. John of the Cross." Wojtyla received the highest possible marks. Though he completed all of his course work for a Doctor of Sacred Theology and with highest honors, he did not receive his degree because he could not afford to pay to have his dissertation printed, as was required by the school. (The degree would be conferred upon him a year later at Jagiellonian University, which did not have the "printed dissertation" requirement, and Wojtyla's doctoral paper would be extolled for its insightful depiction of the "psychological aspects of the experience of faith.")

Father Wojtyla returned to Poland on June 15, 1948.

BACK TO THE MOTHERLAND

When Father Wojtyla left Poland in 1946, the war had just ended and Poland had a so-called coalition government. There was relief, if not hope, in the air. Now the mask of the coalition government had been torn off, revealing the Polish United Workers' Party (PZPR)—the decorative name for the Communists—and the era of good feeling was over. Other countries were now under Communist rule: East Germany, Romania, Czechoslovakia, Bulgaria, and Hungary. Everywhere one turned, the Soviets were running the show, and their agenda had become disturbingly apparent.

In Warsaw Cardinal Hlond was dead; Poland's new primate (religious head) was Bishop Stefan Wyszynski. The forty-seven-year-old Wyszynski was a war hero and a sociologist. He was virtuous and savvy, and he would become a pivotal player in Poland's decades-long effort to oust the Communists. He also would break new political ground by being the first Catholic leader seemingly to agree to coexistence with Communism. His strategy was to work with them at the surface, and defy them underground. As a result, no one but Wyszynski ever knew what Wyszynski was doing. For his fiercely anti-Communist superiors at the Vatican, he was a major thorn.

The Roman Catholic Church's relations with the Soviet Union in the 1950s were subtle and confounding. For example, Archbishop Sapieha of Krakow did not have a close relationship with the Vatican, but he did agree with the Vatican's policy of having no formal commu-

THE BIRTH OF THE VATICAN CITY-STATE

For centuries Italy was divided into states and principalities bound only by Dante's tongue and the Catholic faith. From 1830 to 1870 a movement called *Risorgimento Italiano* sought to unify all of Italy, and in 1861 all the pieces came together—except Rome. Rome was the pope's domain, and though the proponents of Risorgimento Italiano intended to make Rome the capital of the new Italy, Pius IX was adamantly opposed. He could hardly be blamed. Rome was, after all, City of the Popes. Since the beginnings of Christianity, Rome had been the capital of Catholicism, the city of St. Peter and St. Paul, of Mary (more than one hundred churches in Rome are dedicated to the Blessed Mother), of catacombs, martyrs, religious congregations, the Roman curia, seminaries, pontifical universities, masterpieces of religious art and architecture, in essence, the heart and mind of Christ's Church.

But the proponents of *Risorgimento Italiano* were determined. Inspired by Garibaldi, Mazzini, the Carbonist movement, the anticlerical Freemasons, and Voltarian thinkers, the new Italian army "conquered" Rome by firing the single shot of a cannon through the city walls near Porta Pia. Rome became the capital of Italy. The anticlerical minority ruled, confiscating all of the Church's property, revenues, and buildings. The Vatican became a private palace in Rome, under the rule of the Italian government.

As a symbolic protest, four popes of the Roman Catholic Church—Pius IX, Leo XIII, Pius X, and Benedict XV—stayed within the palace walls in self-imposed captivity; they did not even appear on the balcony of St. Peter's to greet the people of Rome on the days of their elections.

Incredibly, this situation lasted for sixty years.

The standoff between the Church and the Italian government was broken when Pius XI, on the day of his election in 1922, greeted an astonished Rome from his balcony at St. Peter's "to bless our dear Italy." That same year, a new government of Fascists had been installed in Italy; the Fascists were young and unestablished, they had no track record

and had not yet exposed their dark side. As a new party, the Fascists needed the recognition of the Church as much as the Church needed its independence to operate. Understanding the opportunity at hand, Pius XI began what would be a seven-year negotiation, painstakingly working to seal an arrangement with the Fascists that would allow the Roman Church to operate free of Italian rule.

On February 11, 1929, the Italian dictator Benito Mussolini and a representative of the pope signed the Lateran International Treaty, which granted the Vatican and the Catholic Church independent status. To amend for its unlawful appropriation of all the country's Catholic churches, the Italian government gave the Church a substantial sum of money. In signing the treaty, the Church was under no obligation to support the Fascist government, and indeed, just a few years later, the Church began its harsh criticism of the Fascists' corrupt ambitions and methods, followed by its unequivocal condemnation of Nazism and Communism in 1937. During World War II, Pius XII openly received at the Vatican Palace enemies of Italy, and Jews, eventually hiding hundreds of them in the palace and in secret locations in Rome. In 1945, at the close of the war, Fascism came to an end.

While the Lateran Treaty has been subject to criticism by some, it was ultimately a simple declaration of independence on the part of the Church. The treaty provided for the Italian government to make restitution to the Church from which it had, in effect, stolen.

The anti-Fascist democratic state, born from the ashes of World War II, incorporated the Lateran Treaty into its Democratic Constitution of 1947, notwithstanding the existence in Italy of the largest Communist party in the West.

The autonomy of the Church, obviously crucial to its mission, has been the key to the enormous achievements of the pontificate of John Paul II, who has used the Church's neutrality and independence to further his cause of correcting social and political injustice throughout the world.

nication of any kind with the Communists. Archbishop Wyszynski of Warsaw, appointed by the Vatican as primate—and therefore number one in the Polish hierarchy—believed it was crucial to establish a quasi-official working relationship with the Communists, and so he did, much to the chagrin of the Vatican and Archbishop Sapieha. While the Soviets were exerting pressure on the Church (they incarcerated seven hundred priests in Poland the moment they took over), they were also willing to deal with Wyszynski with a semblance of respect. Unlike the Germans they saw Poland as a resource to be cultivated, not plundered, and that meant coming to some sort of terms with its overwhelmingly Catholic population. They negotiated with the primate and signed an agreement that gave the Church—basically, the pope—authority over moral and spiritual matters, and the state authority over matters of national interest.

For the Polish Church, even acknowledging that the Communists were in power was a gamble because it meant accepting their legitimacy as a government. But over time, as history would bear out, Wyszynski's agreement would serve the Poles well. It meant that in Poland, unlike all the other Eastern Bloc countries, the Catholic schools would stay open, Catholic press operations could continue, the Catholic University in Lublin would resume classes, and all forms of worship—public and private—would be permitted. The very idea that an outside entity, that is, the pope, might have at least partial authority over the Poles was a huge concession to have extracted. But the Communists gained, too: the Church was expected to encourage civil obedience and adherence to state law, in accordance with sacred Scripture—"render unto Caesar that which is Caesar's."

However practical and ostensibly successful Wyszynski was in dealing with the Communists, the Vatican still didn't like it. To complicate matters, there was some old busi-

CHURCH AND STATE: *Under the Communists, Poles sought solace and consolation from the Church. While the government harrassed the people, the Poles responded with steady, nonviolent resistance, a strategy that ultimately toppled their oppressors.*

ness from World War II between Poland and the Vatican that added to the tension. When Poland was held hostage by the Nazis, Pope Pius XII (who had once served as nuncio to Germany) appeared to some to give more tacit support to the German bishops than to the Polish bishops. Furthermore, after the war when Poland was handed back its western territory from Germany, the Vatican, due to a political hitch, could not replace German bishops with Polish bishops. Ironically, the Polish Church was forced to ally with its Communist government to reestablish official domain over the former German sector.

The politics were exceedingly messy. But they wouldn't have involved a young priest from Krakow and in any event, the young priest judiciously ignored them.

FATHER WOJTYLA

Though Wojtyla will be remembered as one of the most formidable political forces in his century, it was not until he was named an archbishop at the age of forty-four that he showed any awareness of or interest in politics. Before that his interests were scholarly, more reflective than active. He did not find politics distasteful; it was simply his style to work with complete focus on the task at hand.

His first task was somewhat of a surprise. Following his return from the exalted academics of Rome, he was immediately dispatched to serve as a vicar in a pastoral, rough-hewn community southeast of Krakow. Not only were Niegowici's residents mostly uneducated peasants, but the whole region was devastated by mud from recent flooding. Wojtyla's "rectory," which he shared with another priest, had no plumbing or electricity. He shared his front yard with chickens and goats. Many of the parishioners in the outlying villages had not seen a clean shirt for months or a priest in years.

It was a far cry from the Eternal City, but apparently the small town's parish priest was highly esteemed by Sapieha, and this was to be sort of a pastoral crash course, if not a thinly disguised test. Not sur-

prisingly, Father Wojtyla took it on with
enthusiasm and interest. He would travel by
horse cart to any one of the thirteen villages
in the parish and, with his twinkling blue-
gray eyes, respectful manners, and obvious
warmth, he established a remarkable connection with his rural flock. Ironically, as backward as Niegowici was, the locals initially
regarded Wojtyla as someone perhaps to be
pitied; they had never seen a priest with such
frayed clothing nor had they ever known a
priest who, by the appearances of his little
room, had no belongings whatsoever.
However odd he might have struck the
parishioners, they grew quite fond of him. He
devoted much time to the sacrament of reconciliation, sitting in the confessional for
hours, and offering deep understanding and
forgiveness to each penitent. He started a
"Living Rosary" prayer circle for the youth of
the villages. In defiance of the Communists,
he began the building of a church using all
volunteer labor. (It was consecrated in 1958.)
During his short service in Niegowici, he
witnessed thirteen weddings and baptized
forty-eight children. In all, he spent seven months there before Sapieha
summoned him back to Krakow. Apparently he had passed the test.

RARE FAMILY SHOT:
*Karol Wojtyla with a member
of his family, presumed to be
an aunt or a cousin.*

　　Father Wojtyla's next assignment was the antithesis of Niegowici,
the urbane university parish of St. Florian's Church in Krakow. At
twenty-nine years of age, the future pope was surrounded by his own:
Polish intellectuals, artists, actors and actresses, and musicians. Only a
few years earlier he too had been a university student, and he fed off
the vigor of the academy and the energy of the youth who were nearly
his peers. In turn, with his innate brilliance and his Roman education,
Wojtyla himself was a star, and the students took to him unreservedly.
Wojtyla's powerful appeal to young people was probably a mix of his
calm, steady nature; his passion for intellectual discourse; his prowess in

canoeing, hiking, kayaking, and skiing; and the defiant attitude that he had toward the government. Though he was decidedly apolitical, Wojtyla painted the Communists as absurd bureaucrats: dangerous certainly, but also rather buffoonish. The young Poles, already predisposed to question authority, loved it. Once again, Wojtyla established a Living Rosary prayer circle. When he met with the students one on one, they felt they could confide in him frankly, without fear of reprisals. His views were orthodox, but his compassion allowed him to share the teachings of Christ with Christ's love, not the harshness of a cold father. In the midst of the Soviet repression and the gray postwar economy, it is small wonder that Father Wojtyla's blend of hope, mysticism, and intellectualism attracted thousands of young people to retreats and workshops at St. Florian's. In turn, he slept little and devoted every waking moment to helping them sanctify their lives.

Wojtyla's apostolate to Krakow's intellectual and cultural elite was important because of the enormous pressure the Church was getting from the Communists, despite the agreement Cardinal Wyszynski had negotiated. The Church needed respected, compelling priests articulating the faith to counter the Communists' sophisticated anti-Church propaganda. The Communists had created an organization called Pax for priests and influential Catholic lay people patriotic to the so-called new Poland. Some left-leaning priests did join Pax, and those who didn't risked harassment and even arrest.

The success of Pax was bolstered by the government's anti-Church campaign, which accused the Church of favoring the rights of wealthy property owners over those of the working class. In reality, the Polish Church had been the sole champion of the working class for generations. While priests and lay people were buying into the pressure and the propaganda, Wyszynski met the challenge with dignity and equanimity, imploring all Catholics "to pray for those who would persecute us . . . to no one let us repay evil with evil." He ordered all priests not to support anti-Church programs. But under constant pressure from the Soviets, the government continued to tighten its grip. In 1950 they initiated a "census," which in practical terms required all individuals in Poland to turn in their birth and marriage certificates and whatever employment documentation they had. With this "voluntary" dismantling of the old system, the government was able to track every worker, property, and business in the country. The Party also established the "neighborhood committee" system, a Communist trademark, whereby neighbors were grouped into precincts and "self-monitored"— that is, neighbors spied on one another.

Poland once again became a prison.

Even worse, in a remarkably short time, the Communist-led Polish economy went from wartime stagnation to complete paralysis. While the Soviets issued sunny economic reports, goods stopped being pro-

WOJTYLA, THE PHILOSOPHER

I f Karol Wojtyla had not been elected pope, he might have spent the last half of his life addressing the philosophical issues that so enthralled him. Wojtyla's primary area of study was phenomenology, which was founded by a Czech named Edmund Husserl. Husserl's associate Edith Stein, a Jewish academic who converted to Catholicism and became a nun, also ascribed to the phenomenologist point of view. She died at Auschwitz and John Paul II canonized her as a saint in 1998.

Phenomenology is about human perception and reality; in so many words, it asks whether meaningful reality is merely what we perceive. Phenomenologists vary in their approach, but God generally is not part of their equation, given their sense that reality is relative. God presumes absolute truth, whether human beings can perceive it or not. But what Wojtyla was interested in was not so much how our perceptions reveal who we are but how our actions reveal who we are. He took this idea of subjectivity and applied it to what we do, rather than what we think. It was a major stretch, but in translating phenomenology to the world of action, which is a fundamental Catholic ethic, Wojtyla was trying to link Husserl to something—anything—Christian.

Most philosophers who worked with Wojtyla said he had a long way to go, but that with time he could have broken major ground. Instead, he became the most active man of his time.

Father Wojtyla, philosopher

THE OUTDOORSMAN:
Father Wojtyla was an avid cyclist, and spent weekends biking around Poland with his youth groups. Since the Soviets banned organized religious meetings, the teenagers would call him Uncle or Little Uncle so as not to expose him as a priest. Wojtyla had an unusual ability to connect with young people, with whom he had deep, honest discussions about life, death, sexuality, and morality. He was a kindly, nonjudgmental, generous teacher, always guiding the young people to the reality of God's enormous love for them.

duced and services disappeared. A black market emerged, and the Poles, who once prided themselves on their honesty, began to cheat and steal and even betray their neighbors. If the war was awful, the so-called peace wasn't much better.

In Krakow, Father Wojtyla focused on individual souls rather than on the growing economic malaise. He established himself as a sort of chaplain to the intelligentsia in the St. Florian's parish on the Jagiellonian campus, and he was thoroughly comfortable in his role as a priest-father to thousands of people nearly his age. He realized, too, that despite his shy nature, he had pastoral gifts that could be used by God to achieve good.

By 1951, for the first time in his life, Wojtyla sensed that he might have found his true vocation, an apostolate to the intelligentsia. But that year, Cardinal Sapieha died. Certainly it was an emotional blow; Sapieha had nurtured Wojtyla like a son, having recognized the future pope as unusually gifted when he was a mere boy in Wadowice. Sapieha's passing would also provoke another life change for Wojtyla. Before his death, a professor at Jagiellonian, Father Ignacy Rozycki, had told Sapieha that Wojtyla had enormous scholarly potential, and recommended that he be plucked from pastoral work and sent to the university. Sapieha agreed, and called Wojtyla in to inform him that the archdiocese thought him best suited to a scholarly career, that in fact they wanted him to take a two-year leave of absence and pursue a second doctorate in philosophy. Wojtyla might have hesitated at the time, but he certainly would not contradict Sapieha's instruction.

Obviously the archdiocese was taking Father Wojtyla's formation very seriously. He had passed the test of Niegowici. At St. Florian's he had established himself as a friend of the youth, young marrieds, artists, and intellectuals—and he had celebrated 160 wedding masses and baptized 229 souls. Though he had always considered himself contemplative, he now knew that he also had pastoral gifts.

But it had been decided. Father Wojtyla would not leave Krakow, but he would leave his flock and return to the university. He would move in with Father Rozycki, who had already even gone so far as to select Wojtyla's thesis subject: German philosopher Max Scheler's system of ethics.

WOJTYLA, THE SCHOLAR

Whatever hesitation Wojtyla might have had about leaving his pastoral work, it dissipated overnight. Wojtyla made a fluid transition and quickly came to enjoy his work at the university on Scheler, a phenomenologist. Phenomenologists study human perceptions and reality. Wojtyla eventually would become a leading expert in this philosophical school of thought.

As it turned out, the move back to academia was just what Wojtyla needed. For the first time since he was been a child, and for the last time in his life, he was able to establish a routine that included lots of time for athletic and artistic pursuit. He could now engage in his favorite physical activities like kayaking and bicycle riding. He often took students on weekend trips where they would hike and ski, discuss spiritual matters and philosophy, and celebrate Mass. By governmental decree, priests were forbidden to lead youth groups, so the students would call him Little Uncle or Uncle and he would refrain from wearing his clerical collar. Students remember Wojtyla as open, engaging, and nonjudgmental, though he took each student very seriously. The group would sing into the early hours but Uncle would always be up early the next day to bathe and spend time alone in prayer or give spiritual direction to a student. He began to write poetry again. He kept up with his old friends at the Rhapsodic Theater and attended productions whenever he could. He celebrated Mass at St. Catherine's Church. And he pursued his doctorate in philosophy with enormous pleasure and enthusiasm.

While Wojtyla was pondering life's great questions and hiking with young students, the tensions between the Church and the government mounted. In November 1952 the police raided the archbishop's palace in Krakow and arrested Archbishop Sapieha's successor, Archbishop Eugeniusz Baziak, and dozens of priests. Several of the priests were tortured. In Warsaw Primate Wyszynski endured protracted and humiliating negotiations to free them and ultimately was forced to replace Archbishop Baziak with a prelate the Communists believed would be more malleable (eventually Baziak would be reinstated). Priests were accused of consorting with U.S. intelligence agen-

ACTIONS: THE MEASURE OF A MAN

"Each man is the unrepeatable reality of what he is and what he does, of his intellect and will, of his conscience and heart."

—Pope John Paul II, *Redemptor Hominis, 1979*

For ten years, in the midst of everything else, Wojtyla worked on his big book *The Acting Person,* which was published in Polish in 1969. He wanted to establish that an individual is best understood by his actions—rather than the quality of his thinking, argument, or intentions. To do this he attempted to connect Thomism (the theology of St. Thomas Aquinas), phenomenology, and existentialism. Wojtyla's prose had always been on the dense side, but this book, apparently, was unreadable. When he presented it to the professors at Catholic University in Lublin in December of 1970 they respectfully identified the book's flaws; eventually, Wojtyla came to agree that *The Acting Person* failed. Had he accomplished his objective, he would have authored a landmark book in philosophical thought. Instead, it only partially came together. The rejection of his work was no doubt a jarring experience; after all, until then, he had never really failed at anything. He was discouraged, but in the end he was . . . philosophical.

However tepid the response to *The Acting Person* was in Poland, in the United States a Polish-born philosopher named Anna-Teresa Tymieniecka read the book and thought it was brilliant. It dovetailed with her own position as a phenomenologist, and she immediately sought to advance Wojtyla's cause. In 1976 she and her husband, Hendryk Houthakker, hosted Wojtyla in the United States, and arranged for the future pope to speak at Harvard University, where he was very well received. Anna-Teresa Tymieniecka and her husband were ongoing characters in Wojtyla's life. *The Acting Person* was ultimately published in the United States in 1977, though very few copies were sold. An Italian translation from the definitive 1977 edition was published in 1982 by the Vatican publisher (Libreria Editrice Vaticana, Vatican City) and was welcomed in philosophical circles.

cies and Radio Free Europe. In a bold and devastating move, the Communists ruled that henceforth all Catholic clergy appointments had to be government approved.

Wyszynski assessed the impossible situation and responded with subtlety and an iron will. He did not have guns or soldiers, yet he did have a simple but effective communication system: the pulpit. What Poland needed most was hope. Each week every Catholic Church in Poland would receive his written announcements, which were in turn read to parishioners from the pulpit at Sunday Mass. The primate always chose his words carefully, and they were designed to inspire, draw political distinctions, and preach nonviolence. Over the next thirty years the pulpit would be the main source of information for the Polish people. By speaking in parables, myths, and religious double meanings, the primate was able to communicate with his people and his clergy.

FRESH AIR: *For years Wojtyla took his student youth groups on camping and hiking trips and retreats. No matter how late he stayed up with the teenagers, singing and playing the guitar, he would wake before dawn to pray. He served as the spiritual director and counselor to hundreds of young people during the 1940s and 1950s.*

Stalin died on March 5, 1953, and the Party ordered the Church newspaper *Tygodnik Powszechny* to write a positive eulogy. Editor Jerzy Turowicz refused—and the government booted him and his entire staff out of the offices. They were replaced with the so-called patriotic priests of Pax, who basically turned the newspaper into a Communist propaganda organ.

Incredibly, in September, the secret police broke into Cardinal Wyszynski's home and arrested him. He was taken to a remote monastery, where he was put under twenty-four-hour surveillance. He would remain there for three years.

By the end of the year, eight bishops and nine hundred Polish priests would be imprisoned. The Vatican responded by excommunicating Boleslaw Bierut, Poland's nominally Catholic president.

While Father Wojtyla worked on his dissertation, he also ran ethics seminars for students, intellectuals, and clergy. Still, and perhaps amazingly, he avoided politics and did not discuss publicly the anti-Church government and the Polish Church. He began his work on Christian sexuality, and developed an approach that doubtless was shocking for Catholics in his day, unifying the concept of procreation and married love.

In December 1953 Wojtyla's dissertation was accepted by the university, but he did not get his doctorate degree because the government had officially disbanded the faculty of the theology school. Father Wojtyla began to teach and lecture on Catholic social ethics. He continued to ski and hike with his students in the winter, and kayak in the summer.

THE POLISH RESISTANCE

When hard-liner Boleslaw Bierut died, the country's economic deterioration forced the Polish Politburo to turn to Wladyslaw Gomulka, a moderate. Gomulka's first move was to release Cardinal Wyszynski. The moderate Communists understood well that for their regime to

last, they had to have the cooperation of the Polish Church. Wyszynski also knew it. Boldly he negotiated a one-sided deal with Gomulka: all imprisoned priests would be freed, all bishops reinstated, and the church would once again have autonomy in appointing its own bishops. The newspaper *Tygodnik Powszechny* was liberated from its staff of "patriotic priests" and was free to publish. The Church was back.

While he was imprisoned, Wyszynski had done a lot of thinking and planning. Most important, he had created a plan to use the upcoming one thousandth anniversary of the birth of Christianity in Poland as an opportunity to declare symbolically the Church's sovereignty. He initiated a "Great Novena"—a pilgrimage of prayer to Our Lady at the Shrine of the Black Madonna of Czestochowa—which would occur, according to the tradition of the Catholic novena, once a year for nine years. The observance would culminate in 1966 with the millennium anniversary. Though religious activities were still essentially outlawed, Wyszynski used the pulpit to get the word out to more than one million Poles, who, in a stunning display of courage, made the first pilgrimage to the shrine of the Black Madonna in Czestochowa on August 26, 1956. At this gathering, Poles in a single voice rededicated their country to Mary, Mother of God and Queen of Poland, putting all matters—of the individual, family, work, and society—into her holy hands. It was an unparalleled showing of Polish determination and faith.

In the midst of this, Father Wojtyla received an appointment to Catholic University in Lublin, where he was named chairman of the ethics department. He was thirty-six. Lublin was an all-night journey from Krakow, but Wojtyla chose to keep his permanent home in Krakow, where he also served as a chaplain for the medical school at Jagiellonian University and lectured on Christian ethics. He became a popular professor, teaching introductory courses in philosophy and ethics. He also maintained and advanced his interest in human sexuality and

EASTER VIGIL, 1966

*This is a Night above all nights, when
keeping watch at Your grave
we are the Church.
This is the night of strife
when hope and despair do battle within us.
This strife overlays all our past struggles,
filling them all to their depths.
(Do they lose their sense then, or gain it?)
This is the Night, when the earth's ritual attains its
    beginning.
A thousand years is like one night:
the night keeping watch
at Your grave.*

—KAROL WOJTYLA

love, giving open and honest talks to his students about real-life issues. Much of his thinking went into a paper, "Love and Responsibility," which would later be expanded into a book. He also wrote a book called *Catholic Social Ethics.* In addition, he composed poetry and sixteen essays on ethics.

As much time as he spent writing, work with the students truly consumed him. Dressed in his tattered clerical suit and funny shoes, Uncle was still an odd, beloved figure.

BECOMING A BISHOP

When a bishop dies, the Catholic Church often moves with uncharacteristic speed. And so it was somewhat of a shock when Father Wojtyla was called to Krakow by Archbishop Baziak from a youth outing in the mountains. An auxiliary bishop had died, and Archbishop Baziak had chosen him to be the replacement. Wojtyla's response was somewhat measured: he asked to return to his camping trip with the students and celebrate Sunday Mass with them, which he did, putting off what he might have sensed was inevitable: that he was a priest destined for larger things.

Wyszynski, who had to approve Archbishop Baziak's choice, was not enthusiastic about Wojtyla. For one thing, he didn't know him. For another, Wojtyla was a scholar, and Wyszynski had little use for academics. Wojtyla had no administrative experience, and much of a bishop's responsibility fell into that category. He also was a mere thirty-eight—unusually young for such an exalted position. But the appointment went through. Indeed, when the Communists were notified of the appointment, they approved it with a shrug. They figured Wojtyla was just a scholar, probably a leftist, and therefore "harmless."

Wojtyla was ordained bishop on September 28, 1958, at the Wawel Cathedral. Though he had no real family, the crowd of well-wishers was so great that it spilled over and filled the street in front of the cathedral: an immensely diverse collection of students, actors, country parish-

ioners from Niegowici, priest friends, academics, journalists, and nuns. Wojtyla might have been a loner, but he was beloved. He also loved. For his official motto, he took a phrase from St. Louis Marie Grignon de Montfort: *Totus tuus* ("All yours"). He would inscribe his motto on the top right-hand corner of everything he wrote henceforth in dedication to the Blessed Virgin Mary.

It was customary for new bishops to be rewarded with some gifts or privileges. Wojtyla's requests were simple, almost childlike: he asked for a canoe, a separate tent for camping trips, a desk lamp, and a little portable desk so he could work when he traveled. He also wanted his mother's and brother's bodies to be moved from Wadowice to the military cemetery in Krakow, where his father was buried, so his family could be together.

Just a few days after Wojtyla was ordained bishop, Pope Pius XII died. Pope John XXIII was elected, and within months,

WOJTYLA, THE POLITICAL GENIUS: *The future pope had never been directly involved in political matters while he was a priest. When he became bishop, he suddenly found himself charged with defending the Church, which meant protecting it from the Communists. He soon discovered he had remarkable political instincts.*

the Second Vatican Council was called.

In Krakow, Bishop Wojtyla assumed his new role with the same trademark vigor he had applied to every other endeavor in his life. Though he was still relatively young, he was somewhat bent over now, and became a familiar sight on Krakow streets in his worn but neatly pressed cassock, granting each individual who approached him his complete attention. In the early months, much of what he did would remain unchanged: he conducted retreats for various interest groups, such as students, religious, lawyers, physicians, and scientists. He continued to write for *Tygodnik Powszechny* (under a pseudonym) and to celebrate special Masses for the journalists. He lectured on ethics. It was business as usual but with one exception: the government was now watching him, and it was concerned about what it saw.

What the government saw was a bishop who could draw crowds and convey the Catholic message with gravity, clarity, and enthusiasm, and who also was highly regarded by the leadership class. A representative of a Communist front organization, the National Council of Krakow, wrote a heated protest letter to Archbishop Baziak, accusing Wojtyla of disrupting society by distinguishing the interests of believers from nonbelievers. It was a bogus charge but in those tense times a serious one, and it served an important purpose even if it was not what the Party intended. After a lifetime removed from politics, Wojtyla awoke to the realization that as a postwar bishop in Poland, politics was part of his job description. This was a pivotal moment in his life; he was no longer a mere academic and pastor, but a public figure called to serve as the Church's defender.

The Communists' intimidation of Wojtyla produced the opposite of its intended effect. Rather than slowing down his activities, Wojtyla stepped them up, traveling from parish to parish, meeting with priests, nuns, and the faithful.

Wojtyla's approach to the increasing attempts of the government to suppress Catholicism was characterized by his willingness to compromise on logistics but not on principle. His method—without exception—was nonviolence. He would never use a human life as a weapon. He also realized that his power derived from moral authority, and so he fought only those battles that advanced the moral or spiritual good. In one instance, when the government refused a building permit for a church, Wojtyla held outdoor Masses on the construction site, through all weather, week after week. He even celebrated Midnight Mass there, rather than in the elegant Wawel Cathedral. Embarrassed, the government gave in. Bishop Wojtyla understood not only the power of words, but the power of theater. The battle of wills over the bishop's new church would be the first of many dramatic and symbolic political gestures that Wojtyla would instigate to advance the freedom of his people.

In another case, Wojtyla rebuked the Communists with a word. The government forbade Catholics to address priests in the honorific "Father," requiring them instead to refer to priests as "Mister." When parishioners would call him Mister, Wojtyla corrected them, and insisted that all the priests in his diocese do the same. That small measure of defiance had an enormously empowering effect on each parishioner who stood corrected, and on each priest who was required to insist gently upon the truth.

Sometimes Wojtyla didn't weigh the political nuances of his actions, he just tried to solve problems. This had the effect of political genius. When he received word that the government was about to take over the Krakow seminary and make it into a state teachers' training college, he immediately went to the PZPR headquarters and confronted the deputy in charge. No bishop had ever walked into a Communist's office; it just wasn't done. Wojtyla strolled in and called for a meeting, and after the Party functionaries recovered from their shock the two parties worked out a compromise: the seminary would remain a seminary, except that the third floor would loan space to the state teachers' training program. Aware of the importance of the semi-

NOWA HUTA: TO BUILD A CHURCH

All throughout his priesthood, beginning in the rural parish of Niegowici, Wojtyla had encouraged church building. His aim was pragmatic but also symbolic; every time a church went up it was a sign—contrary to Communist plan and the fashionable thinking of the 1960s—that God was *not* dead. Obviously the Communists in Poland did what they could to discourage new churches, and so created a byzantine process for obtaining building permits. Wojtyla's strategy, as always, was nonviolence. Instead of riots or vandalism, he chose to work within the law, often to an extreme. This meant filing for a permit, hundreds and hundreds of times, brilliantly driving the bureaucrats mad with their own game of paperwork. He also would frequently celebrate Mass—rain, shine, or snow—on the proposed site, erecting makeshift crosses. These defiant outdoor Masses put a spotlight on the Communist oppression, and gave the parishioners a sense of empowerment and determination.

The Communists had created a utopian indus-

trial town outside of Krakow called Nowa Huta (New Foundry). Its centerpiece was a steel mill. More than 200,000 Poles were forced to live, shop, and work there, and they could not leave the town without permission. The nearest church was practically a two-hour walk from town. Wojtyla petitioned for a church site for Nowa Huta, and after countless rejections he received approval from the Gomulka government to at least erect a large wooden cross. The petitioning process had taken nearly nine years. To keep the project alive, Wojtyla would hold open-air Masses on the site, celebrating feast days and holy days on the dirt plot. He created numerous congregations within the town, each with an assigned priest, and Mass was celebrated in people's living rooms. Finally, in 1967, the people of Nowa Huta received the much coveted construction permit to build a Roman Catholic Church on ... Karl Marx Avenue.

On May 15, 1977, ten years later, Cardinal Wojtyla consecrated the church at Nowa Huta with a Holy Mass. Some 50,000 Poles attended.

nary to the faithful, Wojtyla let it be known that the Church had prevailed, by leading a special holy procession around the building to rededicate it to the Blessed Virgin, Queen of Poland. It was more political theater, and it worked.

In his "spare" time, Wojtyla continued to write, and expanded his paper *Love and Responsibility* into a book, which was published in 1962. Up to that point the Church's teaching on sexuality had been framed mostly in terms of reproductive function, considered otherwise an impulse to be repressed. The secular West, Wojtyla believed, had also reduced sexuality to its physiological function. For Wojtyla, both views were limited. *Love and Responsibility* presented his conclusions about human sexuality not just in terms of function but in terms of meaning. Human sexuality was not just physiological, he suggested, but psychological and spiritual. A book by a priest that interpreted human sexuality not just as a means of reproduction but also as a way in which to give and receive pleasure in married love was startling and controversial. It would also serve as a profound influence in Pope Paul VI's encyclical *Humanae Vitae* of 1968, which famously restated the Church's ban on artificial contraception while less famously exploring new understandings of marital love.

In 1962 Archbishop Baziak died, and Bishop Wojtyla was appointed on a temporary basis to replace him. He now was the number one acting bishop in Krakow and, in Poland, subordinate only to the primate, Cardinal Wyszynski.

THE SECOND VATICAN COUNCIL

The doctrines of the Roman Catholic Church are set not by the pope, as most people think, but by the bishops in general councils. The first one was held by the Apostles (to Catholics, the first bishops) when they met in Jerusalem circa A.D. 50 to hear Paul's argument on why Gentile converts should not have to follow Jewish law. Other notable councils include the Council of Nicea of A.D. 325, which set the creed by which Christendom lives, and the Council of Trent (1545–63), which launched the Counter-Reformation. And so on January 25, 1959, when Pope John XXIII announced the Second Vatican Council, the twenty-first in the history of the Church, it was a milestone in Catholic history. His agenda was to open the Church and "bring it up to date," a process he called *aggiornamento*. It promised to be a theological and liturgical blood bath.

When Wojtyla arrived in Rome, he made the rounds visiting his Polish acquaintances and other contacts, trying to learn as much as he could about the imminent proceedings. Needless to say, his ability to speak Italian, German, French, Spanish, Polish, Latin, and to a lesser extent, English, gave him an immediate leg up on his more linguistically challenged counterparts.

A good friend of his, Father Andrzej Maria Deskur, a Polish prelate who was running the secretariat in the Vatican for the press and communications, had been appointed press secretary of the Council, putting him in a unique position to drop the word at appropriate moments that in Wojtyla, the new bishop from Poland, the Church had a brilliant moral theologian and independent thinker—in other words, a star. As a result, in the earliest days of the council, almost every commission requested to have Wojtyla as a committee participant. It was an amazing development for a little-known bishop from an Eastern Bloc country.

The Vatican Council began on October 11, 1962, with some 2,800 Council Fathers in attendance. Observers from other Christian denominations were present, along with scribes, auditors, and advisers. The Polish delegation consisted of twenty-five members of the clergy, who came to Rome essentially penniless. (Upon their arrival, a very large check from Polish Catholics in Chicago for transportation, meals, communications, and clerical costs was presented to Cardinal Wyszynksi by Archbishop John Krol of Philadelphia, a Polish American. It was one of dozens of timely and generous gifts that Polish Americans would provide to Polish clergy over the next several years.)

No one had heard of Wojtyla before the council, but before it was over he had established an excellent reputation among his peers. He used his boundless energy to meet with as many of the clergy as he could, soliciting their ideas and views. Though in most cases he knew

the material better than most, he chose mainly to listen. When he spoke, it was to ask questions, and his queries were always penetrating. His ability with languages dazzled. People recall him chatting at receptions with cardinals from all over the world, gliding in and out of each language with ease, and even making jokes in the vernacular.

The daily meetings, which went on for about three months at each of the four sessions, consisted of sometimes endless speeches of varying interest and quality, all spoken in Latin. By late afternoon many of the cardinals and bishops began to grow weary of it all, but Wojtyla, who has a remarkable ability to retain what he reads and hears almost verbatim, was relaxed and alert throughout. Even more astonishing, he displayed his ability to pursue two trains of thought simultaneously. While absorbed deeply in the speeches and papers given by hundreds of

VATICAN II: *Over the course of the Second Vatican Council, Cardinal Wojtyla became known as a progressive intellectual and moral theologian. He led the movement that lifted the Catholic Church from its World War II isolation to its present role as a worldwide champion for human rights. He is pictured here with his fellow cardinals at a meeting in Rome.*

Council Fathers, he simultaneously wrote poems. When he was not writing poems, he was drafting papers or praying—all while taking in every word.

In the days of the Second Vatican Council, Wojtyla was aligned intellectually with the more progressive, change-oriented thinkers. He never wavered on essential dogma but his pastoral sense and his basic concern with the rights and dignity of humankind put him more in the camp of the liberals. He presented two written papers and gave two speeches during the Council. The most influential speech was on the liturgy, the complex of official prayers and holy ceremonies of the Catholic Church. Wojtyla made the case that the liturgy should be more understandable and supported the use of local language in Church liturgy to increase understanding for the faithful. (Up to that point, the Mass was always spoken in Latin, in every Catholic church, all over the world.) On this issue, he was at odds with the conservative faction of the council, but the view he supported ultimately did prevail.

The following June, Pope John XXIII died. Giovanni Battista Cardinal Montini was elected to the office, and would be known to the world as Pope Paul VI. To insiders, Paul would also be known as the man who discovered Karol Wojtyla.

In October 1963 Wojtyla returned to Rome for the second session of the Second Vatican Council. This time he brought researchers, including two women, because he was determined to involve the laity in church matters. He worked on the *Lumen Gentium* Declaration on the Dogmatic Constitution of the Church. He was interested in the radical semantic insistence that "God's people" figure preeminently in the draft of the Vatican II document, over and above "Church hierarchy." His argument was that the Church is God's people, not merely a hierarchy of power. Wojtyla did not want to reduce the monarchical powers of the pope, but he was calling for a reenvisioning of the Church, a change in emphasis and empowerment, rather than organizational structure.

Wojtyla expressed another concern at the second session—ecumenism, or the reunification of all Christians—which he said must be developed "on an unprecedented scale." In Poland, practicing ecumenism with ease, he hosted regular dinners for Protestants of every variety as well as Jews to discuss what they could do to help each other

POPE PAUL VI: *Toward the end of his papacy, Pope Paul VI spent more and more time with Cardinal Wojtyla, turning to him for companionship as well as political and theological insight. Many credit Paul VI as the man who "discovered" Karol Wojtyla. Even today, Pope John Paul II has called Paul VI "my teacher and father."*

as men and women of God. Significantly, the ecumenical dialogue he established in Poland unified the leadership class, thus making it a more formidable adversary against the Communists. The call for ecumenism would stay with him all through the 1960s and '70s, and ultimately would be a feature of his papacy.

CARDINAL WYSZYNSKI

Wojtyla reveled in the Vatican Council, but for Cardinal Wyszynski it was a distraction. At the moment, Wyszynski was much more concerned about the fate of his country than the Church universal. Wyszynski's people were in danger, and he correctly saw himself as their chief defender. But when the Council was over and all the delegates returned to Poland, Wyszynski was under serious pressure to recommend a permanent archbishop of Krakow, and this presented a problem: he did not want to nominate Karol Wojtyla.

Wyszynski had never connected with Wojtyla. He considered Wojtyla a bishop of the elite. Certainly intellectuals, students, and journalists adored Wojtyla, but the future pope was from a decidedly humble background and was extremely accessible. Wojtyla's door, quite literally, was always open. By contrast, it was almost impossible to get in to see Wyszynski; he surrounded himself with layers of bureaucracy and protocol. Wyszynski may not have been a bishop from the elite, but he certainly behaved like one. As a further twist, most of the clergy in Krakow, who were largely intellectuals themselves, regarded Wojtyla as a worker-class priest. Wojtyla's giant intellect would eventually win him the respect of the Krakow clerical elite, and deepen Wyszynski's distrust.

Wojtyla never expressed his feelings about Wyszynski, and in public always treated him with deep respect. Yet Wyszynski could not be pacified. At a meeting where Wyszynski had been lecturing he noticed that Wojtyla was sitting in the very back row, reading rather than listening to the primate. Insulted, the cardinal asked Wojtyla to review what Wyszynski had said thus far in his speech. To the amazement of everyone, Wojtyla repeated almost verbatim what the primate had said from the very beginning of the lecture. Wyszynski was not amused.

The procedure for installing an archbishop at that time was for the primate to make his formal recommendation and then for the Communists to give their "blessing," so to speak, with the final nod coming from Rome. Wyszynski proposed several candidates. One at a time, each was rejected by the government. Finally, when he had essentially run out of candidates, Wojtyla's name surfaced. Without a moment's hesitation, the "left-leaning" worker-priest was approved.

Once again, the Communists miscalculated. In Wojtyla's files they found an elaborate report on the Krakow seminary episode, when the state had intended to take over the Krakow seminary for its teacher training program. Wojtyla had been willing to talk to them and work out a compromise (the Communists got one floor, Wojtyla got the rest of the building). Somehow, though they had come out losers in the deal, Wojtyla seemed like a man they could work with. Indeed, they were so pleased with the notion that they might have in Wojtyla a "Church ally" that they accepted him unequivocally.

They would live to regret that decision.

With the government's blessing and the pope's approval, Wojtyla, at the age of forty-three, was invested as the archbishop of Krakow on January 13, 1964.

Wojtyla had never aspired to live in a palace.

For his installation, he wore the traditional gilded vestments—theatrically and ceremoniously and with visible humility—but most of

OPENING THE CHURCH:
Paul VI opened the Church to people from all over the world, breaking precedent by traveling abroad numerous times. His international vision laid the groundwork for what would be the new face of the Roman Catholic Church: yellow, brown, black, red, and white. These changes transformed the College of Cardinals to the extent that it was mathematically possible, in 1978, for a "foreign" (non-Italian) pope to be elected.

RUNNING THE POLISH CHURCH: *Though they were not particularly close during the postwar years, both Cardinal Wyszynski and Cardinal Wojtyla devoted themselves to liberating the Polish people from their Soviet oppressors. The two men conferred often once Wojtyla was elected pope. It was Wyszynski who reaffirmed Wojtyla's intention to take the name John Paul II.*

the time, while he was archbishop, Wojtyla wore his crumpled hat and neatly pressed but faded cassock. His shirts had been mended so many times they were nearly patchwork. If he received a coat for a gift, he gave it away. In fact, though he received gifts continually, he gave almost all of them away, not for a lack of gratitude, but because he had no understanding of accumulation. It didn't occur to him to "own things."

Eventually he moved into his exquisite accommodations, but instead of occupying the grand master bedroom, he slept in a small side bedroom. In the mornings, after Mass, he worked at a small desk behind the altar rather than the sweeping archbishop's office. In the afternoons, he would pray in his private chapel, sometimes on the floor, face down, in the shape of a cross.

Archbishop Wojtyla, the follower of St. John of the Cross, understood that mysticism was not oblivion. The ornate palace may not have interested him, but he knew how to use its power. In the spirit of his mentor Cardinal Sapieha, Wojtyla immediately began to conduct a massive secret seminarian program and smuggling operation, unbeknownst to the governments of both Poland and Czechoslovakia. Young men from Czechoslovakia, which had suffered a complete ban on religion, made their way across the border to study undercover for the priesthood with Wojtyla. Eventually he also trained and secretly ordained priests from Lithuania and the Ukraine, all of whom risked imprisonment and a death sentence for the pursuit of their vocations. Wojtyla smuggled more than people: Bibles, rosaries, and spiritual works suddenly began appearing in Russia and the Eastern Bloc countries where Catholicism was forbidden. Wojtyla, by personal experience, knew all the mountain passes of Poland, and had "hikers" and "mountain climbers" take goods to the border to safe houses, where they would be stored until a pickup could be arranged. Many of the goods that Wojtyla distributed came from Catholic friends in France, Belgium, and Italy. Substantial funding came from Polish-American immigrants in the United States. "Tour groups" from other countries would come loaded down with Bibles and theological texts for the secret seminarians—all requested by Wojtyla. The many friendships he had made during the Second Vatican Council sessions and his tours of Europe would not only support

efforts to train priests but would play an important role in feeding and clothing the Poles, and ultimately in toppling the regime.

Wojtyla also nurtured the quasi-free press that Cardinal Sapieha had so presciently created with *Tygodnik Powszechny* and *Znak*. It is nothing short of remarkable that such independent media were allowed to exist in a Soviet Bloc country, and Wojtyla understood fully their importance to an eventual Polish liberation.

In the fall of 1964 Wojtyla returned to Rome for the third session of the Vatican Council. This time he was even better recognized as an important moral theologian, and he spoke again on the crucial importance of ecumenism and the importance of involving the laity in the workings of the Church. He shocked the Council Fathers by being the first speaker ever to address the convocation with a greeting to his "brothers *and sisters*"—paying homage to the women who were present.

Most significantly, Wojtyla wrote a lengthy paper on how the Catholic Church should relate to the world at large. He defined not only for the Church but also for his future papacy the theme by which history will remember him: human rights. For a man whose people

JOHN PAUL, THE POLYGLOT

Karol Wojtyla began acquiring foreign languages at a very young age. By the time he graduated from high school, he could speak and write Polish, Greek, Latin, and German. During the war, while he worked as a manual laborer and acted and directed underground patriotic theater, Wojtyla engaged a tutor to teach him French. When he became enamored with the writings of mystical saints, he learned Spanish by studying a German-Spanish dictionary, so he might read St. John of the Cross in the original.

The future pope acquired passable Italian and English when he attended the seminary in Rome to obtain his doctorate in theology. He is now, of course, fluent in both languages. In seminary he also studied Hebrew, though he did not fully master it.

Later in life, he learned Portuguese and most Slavic languages. Still, when he goes to address a nation whose language he has not yet mastered, he takes weeks to prepare with a tutor so as to make small talk with dignitaries and to punctuate his speeches with important sentences in the native tongue. When he cried out in Japanese, "Never again, Hiroshima," the people of that non-Christian nation wept.

In his address of December 25, 1998, *Urbi et Orbi* (To the City and to the World), the pope greeted his flock with "Merry Christmas" in fifty-six different languages, so virtually the whole world could understand his message of joy.

had lived through Nazi occupation and Soviet domination, with little support from Rome, the cause of human rights was primary. During World War II, Mother Church, perhaps out of naïveté or ignorance, behaved as a provincial Italian political entity, employing few of her huge spiritual resources at a time when the world most needed her. For Wojtyla, it was crucial that the Church be ready and willing to speak out and act whenever and wherever human rights were violated, whether for Catholics or non-Catholics. He did not want to be part of "an isolated Church" ever again.

A few weeks after the council was adjourned, Wojtyla was summoned to a meeting with Pope Paul VI. It was the beginning of an unusual, affecting relationship between two very private, cerebral men. Wojtyla's personality not only meshed with the pope's, but the pope understood Wojtyla in a unique way, having worked in the Nunciature of Poland. Paul VI was an aristocrat, but he was devoted to the cause of the worker, and this intellectual worker-priest from Poland was a man after his own heart.

The final session of the Second Vatican Council convened in September 1965. By now, Karol Wojtyla of Wadowice, Poland, had established himself as a major force on the Catholic world stage.

Wojtyla's hand could be seen in many of the documents, principal among them the declaration on religious liberty that the Catholic Church now insisted should be a guarantee for all, regardless of religious affiliation. His vision was not for a new Church, but for a Church with a new and larger role. For the first time the Roman Catholic Church pledged to work for the rights all of men and women to worship according to their conscience, freely without government interference. For the first time, a Church Council was not about doctrine and devotion as much as it was about the role of the Church in the outside world—and what it could do to benefit humanity, not just spiritually but on every level.

Whatever influence Wojtyla had in convincing the Second Vatican Council to tackle the problem of human rights, it was being played out in Poland in living color. The Polish Church had become a political heavyweight, using spirituality and hope as its weapons. For nine years

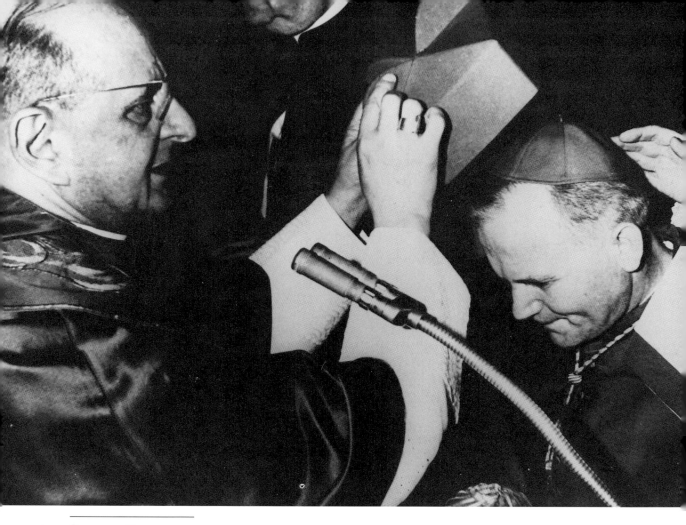

CARDINAL KAROL WOJTYLA: *Before he died, Pope Paul VI made Wojtyla a cardinal. He is pictured here placing the traditional red cardinal's hat on Wojtyla.*

Cardinal Wyszynski had led Poles in prayer in his extraordinary Great Novena. Easter Sunday 1966—the one thousandth anniversary of the founding of Christianity in Poland—had finally arrived, and Cardinal Wyszynski's dream had unfolded nearly according to plan. The government had dreaded this day but wisely decided not to underscore its significance by banning the religious celebration.

To commemorate the anniversary, Wyszynski intended for the faithful to dedicate themselves to Mary, Patron Saint of Poland. This clearly defied the Communists' insistence that no person, place, or thing—including God and Mary—could have a claim on the people's allegiance in a Marxist system.

The centerpiece event was the Mass of Jubilee at Czestochowa, home to the revered image of the Black Madonna. Wyszynski naturally had hoped that Pope Paul would be able to come to celebrate the Mass and the Polish clergy had lobbied hard for permission that never came.

The Polish bishops did not let that detail go unnoticed. At each Mass an empty chair with the pope's photograph was displayed prominently, a reminder of his absence.

Though many insiders knew that Cardinal Wyszynski was not close to Archbishop Wojtyla, the two shared the altar. Wojtyla con-celebrated the Mass, and Wyszynski delivered the homily—presenting a united front to Polish Catholics and to the government. Over the course of the year, Wojtyla would celebrate fifty-three solemn masses dedicated to the jubilee, in parishes throughout Poland.

WOJTYLA'S POLITICAL GENIUS

It was the mid–1960s. Like their counterparts in the United States, students in Poland were becoming politically active. But there the similarity ended: the U.S. students were seeking left-minded solutions to the Vietnam War and their perception of the "Establishment," while the Poles were trying to shake off the totalitarian left. The U.S. students primarily represented the intellectual elite and had little if any connection with the common worker. In Poland, by contrast, the students and workers were essentially united and eventually formed a powerful advisory organization to link the two groups. Called Committee for the Defense of Workers (KOR), this organization, along with *Tygodnik Powszechny* and Wojtyla's progressive wing of the Catholic Church, would serve as invaluable resources to the Solidarity Trade Union Movement and ultimately Poland's liberation. While many of the Polish students were socialists or even watered-down Communists, none of them wanted the Soviets controlling their country. What they wanted first and foremost was freedom.

Wojtyla also served the cause of Polish liberation by organizing his Catholic parishioners on a grassroots level into committees designed to address social reform. These "synods" not only increased lay participation as prescribed by Vatican II, but served as a unique structural counterpoint to the restrictive government and boosted the morale of the people immensely. The synods were the only place in Poland where the people had a voice.

Wojtyla created a staggering number of these synods—more than five hundred in all. They were each assigned to a specific problem facing the people in his diocese. By using Catholic principles that happened to overlap the Communist model, the committees were able to make intelligent recommendations to the government—a number of which were accepted and implemented. Wojtyla was especially concerned about the plight of families, and appointed committees to work out the logistics of awarding pensions to stay-at-home-mothers, creating a model for preschool day-care centers for children of working mothers (a new concept at the time), granting bonuses for professionals who worked with special-needs children, part-time and flex-time hours for working parents, and bringing improvements to orphanages. These ideas were later presented to Parliament and instituted, with remarkable success.

THE IMPORTANCE OF PAUL VI

A month before his forty-seventh birthday, Archbishop Wojtyla went to Rome and Pope Paul IV met with him privately. It was the second time in three years that they had spoken face to face, though Wojtyla had communicated with the pope routinely on various matters about Poland and the Second Vatican Council. Pope Paul VI was an extremely intelligent and contemplative character. He deliberated slowly on important decisions, and sometimes received criticism for this, although history may show that this characteristic served the Church well. He was devoted to world peace, and pleaded repeatedly for an end to the Vietnam War, taking his message to an international venue at the United Nations. He had anguished over the Church's position on artificial birth control and appointed countless commissions to advise him, withholding his judgment until he finally published his extraordinary document *Humanae Vitae.* Over the next several years Paul VI called for private

WOJTYLA, THE FAMILY MAN

"The family is the sanctuary of life."
—Pope John Paul II, *Centesimus Annus*

For Wojtyla, who was fully orphaned by age twenty, family is at the core of the "civilization of love," an expression coined by Pope Paul VI and prized by Pope John Paul II. From his early days in Krakow as a priest, Wojtyla devoted himself to the family; he developed a program for marriage preparation, identified principles for a strong and happy marriage, and explored marital sexuality. Though he was raised essentially as an only child, he acquainted himself with principles of child rearing so he could discuss these vital, practical, everyday realities with his parishioners.

In many ways Wojtyla was ahead of his time. Sociology and psychology were burgeoning quasi-sciences, and he used insights from both fields to help his parishioners. His standards for parenting were radical. As early as the 1950s he was explicit that both the mother *and the father* were expected to nurture and care for the children. He did not like economic forces that forced both parents to work, but he supported the idea of women working out of choice, viewing work as an expression of creativity as well as a means of earning income. At the same time, the future pope assigned the highest value to the role of child rearing; he was pushing for pensions for full-time, stay-at-home mothers.

Long before they existed, Wojtyla advocated day-care centers for working families, with special emphasis on preschool education. He promoted special programs for working with children with disabilities at a young age, and giving incentives to special education teachers and also to the parents of children with special needs. When he became bishop, he created the Institute of the Family in Krakow to help people deal with problems of alcoholism, unwanted pregnancies, and marital conflicts.

Wojtyla also created a group called S.O.S. Cardinal Wojtyla to provide unwed mothers who opted not to have abortions with prenatal care and support for up to a year from the birth of the baby.

IL PAPA: *Long before he became pope, Wojtyla was a profamily activist, calling for social and political support of innovative programs that helped keep families healthy, happy, and together.*

Familes would "adopt" unwed mothers and help the new families with all of their needs.

As pope he created the Pontificate Council for the Family, so that family policy and issues could be studied and recommendations could be made. The Council is also devoted to the plight of abandoned children and the development of curricula for marriage preparation. John Paul II has encouraged bishops worldwide to influence public policy on family concerns, advocating incentives that will keep families together, such as tax breaks, regulation of work hours, and special housing assistance for families in need.

meetings with Wojtyla almost a dozen more times, an unprecedented relationship for a non-Italian. (To this day, Wojtyla refers to Paul VI as his "teacher and father.") The archbishop of Krakow almost became a fixture at the Vatican, and more than one insider sensed that Paul might be engaging in the audacious act of grooming a non-Italian for the papacy.

One indication of Wojtyla's status was the invitation he received in 1976 from Paul VI to conduct a Lenten retreat for the pontiff and some eighty members of the Curia, many of whom were cardinals. At the time Paul was not only emotionally drained from controversy, including criticism from both liberals and conservatives on the Church's ban on artificial birth control, but was losing his physical strength. To prepare for the retreat, Wojtyla created one for himself, spending days in prayer and meditation. When he emerged, he had written a series of meditations later published as *A Sign of Contradiction*.

Pope Paul VI's respect and affection for Wojtyla was obvious to most insiders, but it became apparent to the world when he announced that Wojtyla was to be named a cardinal.

Archbishop Wojtyla received his red skull cap in the Sistine Chapel on June 26, 1967. He was a mere forty-seven years old.

MODERN MAN: *Wojtyla always had been uninterested in material acquisition, but he was sophisticated and adept in his use of electronics, media, and technology to advance the ancient teachings of his 2,000-year-old Church.*

CARDINAL WOJTYLA

Cardinal Wojtyla's world, officially, was now *the* world. He no longer was to restrict his concerns to the needs of his diocese and his beloved Poland but to the universal Roman Catholic Church of one billion souls. He did so with the energy and productivity of a giant, working eighteen to twenty hours a day. He also began what was clearly an initiation process, if not for the papacy, then at least for an even more significant role in the Vatican.

As cardinal, he began to travel to new places: the United States (twice), Canada, Australia, New Zealand, and New Guinea. But often it seemed like he never left Poland. In each country he would seemingly meet with every Polish expatriate he could find—and they were

I STILL HEAR

When I think—my Country—I still hear
The swishing scythe, it strikes the wall of wheat,
Merging into one profile with the arched sky; the
light stoops.

Then harvesters come and cast the monotony of
sound
against that wall
in the violent loops of their gestures. And they cut—
they cut.

—KAROL WOJTYLA

everywhere. In the United States, John Cardinal Krol of Philadelphia, whose parents were born in Poland and who became a cardinal at the same time as Wojtyla, put Wojtyla in touch with literally thousands of Polish-Americans. Wojtyla loved meeting his fellow Poles all over the world and was constantly being torn away from conversations he didn't want to end (as a result, he always seemed to be running late). Since one in five U.S. Catholics is of Polish descent, Wojtyla was welcomed like a monarch by Poles all over the United States. When tensions escalated in Poland in the late 1970s and '80s, these expatriate Polish Catholics, many of whom Wojtyla had met on his travels, would provide the main financial and logistical support to their homeland in its fight to restore its freedom.

In 1970 Gomulka's reign came to an end. In the port of Gdansk, workers went on strike, protesting an increase in food prices just a few weeks before Christmas. The streets were filled with protesting workers until, finally, the town mayor brought a measure of calm, and convinced the strikers to return to work. Many of them showed up the next morning, but in a horrific moment, the government soldiers, thinking it was another strikers' demonstration, opened fire on the workers, who were stuck behind a locked fence and had nowhere to flee. Dozens of the men were slaughtered and thousands injured. The botched operation was blamed on Gomulka, and a new puppet was brought into lead Poland, a career bureaucrat named Edward Gierek. Gierek would name General Wojciech Jaruzelski as his minister of defense.

Gierek began his new administration in a conciliatory mode, much like his predecessor, Gomulka, only this time the Poles knew the drill. He made the political rounds, visiting with workers all over the country, "consulting" with the people about their grievances and needs. He presented himself as new blood, but when food supplies ran out, he followed the Gomulka model and immediately raised prices 39 percent. The Poles were outraged and he immediately lowered them.

Some 2,500 Poles—including all the principal intellectual leaders of the workers' aid
group, KOR—were jailed, and a riot ensued.
Church officials pleaded for the jailed workers to be released and for some kind of compromise. Gierek decided to take his frustration out on the Catholic hierarchy and so his
compromise was this: the government would
roll back food prices but priests and other
clergy could no longer communicate in writing, not even in letters or memos. The maga-
zine *Znak* and the newspaper *Tygodnik
Powszechny* were banned. Gierek wanted the
Church out of his life.

BLESSING HIS FLOCK:
*The future pope blessed the
Polish workers in this
Krakow church, while
encouraging them to seek
non-violent solutions to the
government's relentless
political pressure.*

On August 6, 1978, Pope Paul VI died of a
heart attack at age eighty. However controversial, his legacy was extraordinary: In his fifteen years as pope, he had completed the Second
Vatican Council, established a diplomatic approach to the Communist
East, opened the Church doors wide to the Third World, and issued
Humanae Vitae. Over the years Cardinal Wojtyla probably had more
private audiences with the pope than any non-Italian. Paul's death was
not a surprise; still, Wojtyla grieved for his friend and father figure.

A week after the pope's death, Cardinal Wojtyla arrived in Rome
for his first conclave.

JOHN PAUL I

Many of the cardinals who were gathered in Vatican City for the conclave were, like Wojtyla, newly elevated to the red hat. Escorted by
acolytes and chamberlains, they found themselves bound by ancient
protocol in a ritual of election dominated by precedent and led by
members of the Curia. Strangers to one another, they were naturally

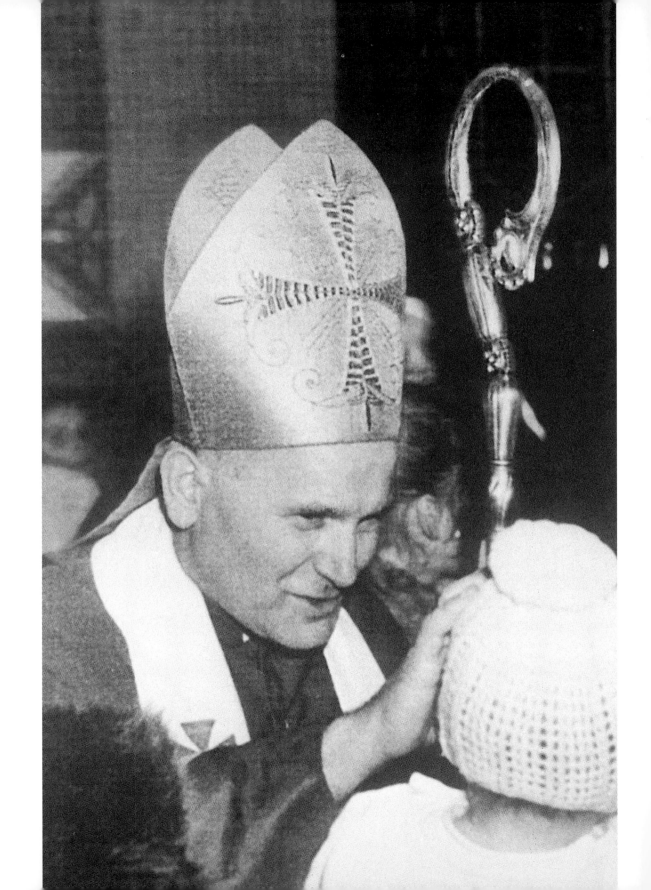

dependent on the helpful advice of their more experienced colleagues, who were primarily Italian, in keeping with the College's long history as an almost exclusively Italian institution.

Steeped in tradition, the conclave was a sign of permanence to a Church that had been deeply shaken by the Second Vatican Council. Paul VI may have been brilliant and saintly, but his thoughtfulness had often been seen as indecision and his aristocratic reserve as detachment. He had visibly suffered from the controversies of his reign and in later years—rightly or wrongly—had come to project a Church under siege.

Now the Church needed a more pastoral, if not avuncular, figure in the papacy. On the first two ballots, no front runner emerged. Wojtyla even got a couple of votes, which were no doubt cast as a compliment, since it had been 456 years since the Church had elected a non-Italian pope, and of course in the nineteen-hundred-year history of the Church, there had never been a pope from Poland. On the third ballot, the cardinals elected Albino Luciani, the warm, simple cardinal from Venice. In honor of John XXIII and Paul VI, Luciani took the name John Paul I. He was installed on September 3, 1978, and was immediately hailed in the media as "the smiling pope." He had never been a strong man, but the huge task of running the Church overwhelmed him, mentally and physically.

He died in his sleep on September 28, just twenty-three days later.

When Cardinal Wojtyla received word of Pope John Paul I's death, friends recall his taking the news with a cosmic sigh. He asked his driver to take him to the edge of the woods at Kalwaria, where he sat in his car and did paperwork, occasionally staring out the window at the place where hundreds of times he had walked and prayed the Stations of the Cross. He spent the next few days getting his affairs in order. He bought a round-trip ticket. Yet in hindsight, he behaved like someone who knew he would not be back.

FUTURE POPE: *John Paul I's sudden death just weeks after he had been elected pope stunned the world. Cardinal Wojtyla grew silent upon hearing the news. He tidied up his desk, and tended to all of his unfinished business in Krakow. He bought a round-trip ticket to Rome, but never used it. When he returned to his beloved Poland in 1979, it would be as Pope John Paul II.*

HEAVEN AND EARTH

✦

1978 TO PRESENT

Tu es Petrus, et super hanc petram
aedificabo Ecclesiam meam.

*(You are Peter, the rock on which I will
build my Church.)*

—MATTHEW 16:18

HABEMUS PAPAM!
WE HAVE A POPE!

MODERN PARADOX: *The new Polish pope, though brilliant and savvy, was not a man of the world. Yet overnight he became a celebrity.*

Once again, the cardinals walked two by two in solemn procession through the doors of the Sistine Chapel to take up their now-familiar stations. They had gathered only five weeks before and, although nothing had changed, everything was different.

These cardinals now knew one another.

They had heard one another speak, had assessed each other over sips of tea, had shared meals together, perhaps politely corrected one's broken Latin or advised another of ways to aid a favorite charity. They had much in common. Each was a prince of the Church, a medieval title that carries modern precedence in rank, both socially and diplomatically. Each had surrendered his national passport on accepting the red hat; their new papers carried the white and gold of Vatican City, signifying that the bearer was a Roman and therefore a citizen of the world. Each one of them, probably from childhood, had dedicated his life to Christ.

Their dissimilarities were more astonishing than their similarities. As they looked from their narrow stall seats to the rows on the opposite side, they could see how radically Paul VI had reshaped the Sacred College: brown faces, black faces, yellow faces, Americans, Australians, Indians. During the last conclave's balloting, as the cardinals stepped from their stalls one by one to deposit their slips of paper in the chalice at the altar, the College's new breadth became glaringly apparent: Italians no longer held their ancient majority. In fact, only 56 of the 110 members of the College eligible to vote were from Western Europe.

A POLISH POPE!: *In a sense, Karol Wojtyla perfectly suited the needs of the modern Catholic Church. A relatively youthful fifty-eight, he was authentically all things to all cardinals: humble, brilliant, mystical, pragmatic, private, and pastoral. A poet, philosopher, and actor, Wojtyla was also an athlete. Amazingly, he spoke eight languages fluently.*

Not only were the Italians now in the minority, but they had few promising candidates. Only weeks before, with the election of Cardinal Albino Luciani of Venice (John Paul I), the college had run through all the possible nominees and the list of potential Italian popes had been a short one. Besides Luciani, only two other Italians had surfaced: Cardinal Giuseppe Siri of Genoa, a conservative who had tried to block many of the changes of Vatican II, and Cardinal Giovanni Benelli

of Florence, a moderate with mostly bureaucratic experience. In the past conclave, Siri had only amassed about a quarter of the votes needed to be elected, so there was a question about the depth of his support. Benelli's support was even less organized but he was young, and in the wake of John Paul I's sudden death, age would be an important consideration.

The last conclave had been so recent it made this one seem virtually a continuation. The cardinals had heard reasons why one candidate was to be preferred over another; they had learned code words that distinguished one as too militant and another as too soft. And although the newer members had been unsure of themselves and deferential, they formed a fragile consensus on the kind of pope they wanted. Above all, they wanted a shepherd, a pastor like the smiling John Paul I, whom they had managed, almost by accident, to elect.

As the cardinals arrived in Rome from their far-flung homelands, Cardinals Siri and Benelli would doubtless have been correct in presuming that they were the candidates from whom the next pope would be chosen. Then, as so often happens, great events were interrupted by a minor scandal. In an interview he thought would not be published until after the conclave, Cardinal Siri made remarks about John Paul I and the Second Vatican Council that were lacking in enthusiasm, if not openly critical. The newspaper released the story *early,* reportedly at the prodding of friends of Cardinal Benelli. The embarrassment on all sides was profound, the effects devastating.

For eight hundred years, not counting the brief reign of Holland's Adrian VI in 1522 (like John Paul I he lasted less than a year) all the popes and most of the cardinals had been Italian. Now that Cardinals Siri and Benelli had lost their momentum, an extraordinary question loomed over Rome: Would the next pope be an Italian?

Even before the scandal, over the telephone in commiserating on John Paul I's sudden death, or in private stopovers on their way to the funeral and the conclave, many cardinals had already been broaching the delicate question. Franz Cardinal König of Vienna, for one, let it be known privately to a few of his colleagues that over the years he had become increasingly taken with the manner and intelligence of the young cardinal from Poland, Wojtyla. He was especially impressed with

SISTINE CHAPEL: *The conclave takes place in the Sistine Chapel, amidst Michelangelo's magnificent frescoes, including* The Last Judgment, *pictured here. However tempted one might be to linger among these masterpieces, the accommodations are not designed for comfort. Each cardinal is given a makeshift cell containing a thin cot, a hard chair, and only the most basic necessities. Under these conditions, they elect Christ's representative on earth.*

SMOKE SIGNAL: *As is tradition, thousands of the faithful wait in St. Peter's Square to be among the first to learn the identity of the new pope. After each day's vote a signal is sent from the palace. If no pope has yet been chosen, black smoke greets the crowd. When a pope is elected, white smoke is sent up, as seen in this photograph taken upon Karol Wojtyla's election to the papacy.*

the ease with which he dealt with the Communists while serving his people's needs. When König suggested the idea of Wojtyla to two or three of his colleagues, he received a tepid response at first, but no one actually said no. Once in Rome, König began mentioning Wojtyla more and more.

Mentions, open reflections, circular conversations, the expression of "concerns," homilies given during Masses, even prayers said aloud over meals—these are the media by which the cardinals test the waters and try to discern the will of the Holy Spirit in the election of a pope. In the days and hours before the second conclave, even as the cardinals arranged themselves in ranks by seniority for the procession into Michelangelo's frescoed chapel, a movement beneath the surface began to swell. Perhaps, just perhaps, it was time for a "foreign" pope.

THE VOTE

When Cardinal Wojtyla first arrived in Rome, he met with his dear friend Bishop Deskur, who over the years had introduced Wojtyla to hundreds of important figures in the Catholic hierarchy. Before the conclave Deskur hosted some small gatherings for Wojtyla, reacquainting the cardinal from Krakow with many of his peers. Wojtyla was not naïve. He knew that he was being evaluated as a papal candidate but he engaged in the process with humility. Whatever sense he had of his imminent election is known only to Wojtyla, but those around him say that he appeared to be weighted down, somber, and pensive. Many believe that he knew long before anyone that he would be the next pope.

The day before the conclave, Bishop Deskur was suddenly hospitalized with a heart attack. Wojtyla was desolate. Deskur was one of Wojtyla's closest friends and allies; they had history and common roots. It was Deskur who had quietly, respectfully promoted Wojtyla's candidacy to the cardinalate. Whatever ambivalence Wojtyla might have had about his possible election must have been cast aside with his friend's life in danger. The future pope prayed at Deskur's bedside until the conclave began.

It convened with the full splendor of the Roman Church on October 14, 1978.

Wojtyla entered the sacred precincts of the conclave, in the core of the Vatican Palace, and deposited his few belongings into Cell 91. The heavy doors of the conclave were shut behind the elector cardinals and locked. Like his brethren, Wojtyla was assigned by lottery to a makeshift cell, furnished with a thin cot, a lamp, a trash can, and a kneeler. On a table was a water pitcher, a hand towel, and a bar of soap. At the ringing of a bell, he returned to the Sistine Chapel, to his assigned bare wooden stall with its stiff, straight-backed chair for the voting sessions.

The voting process is quite simple: each day, up to four votes are taken until a clear majority is reached. All the cardinals who are eligible to vote are given a white card on which the elector is to carefully print his choice. Once all the ballots are received they are read aloud, one at a time, so the cardinals may keep a running tally. In 1978 the number

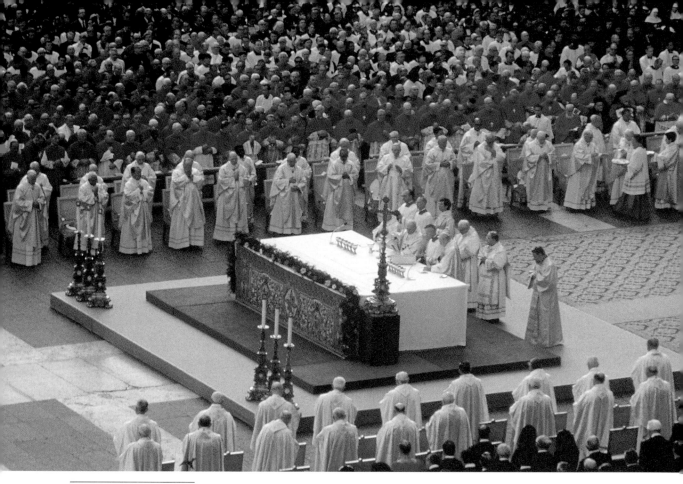

CORONATION: *At his coronation, John Paul II knew that his Polish compatriots watching television and listening to the radio would be waiting for a special word. He spoke to them directly: "What shall I say? Everything that I could say would fade into insignificance compared to what my heart feels, and your hearts feel, at this moment. So let us leave aside words. Let there remain a great silence before God, a silence that becomes prayer." This photograph shows the 1978 ceremony outside of St. Peter's Basilica, viewed electronically by millions all over the world.*

of votes needed to win was seventy-five—two-thirds plus one vote.

On the first day, though the cardinals voted four times, they were unable to come up with a pope. Wojtyla reportedly got a few votes, not many; most of the votes were parceled out between the two Italian front runners, but their support was decidedly lacking.

At the end of the first day of the October 1978 election, thousands of the faithful gathered at St. Peter's Square in hopes of seeing their new Supreme Pastor. Instead, they saw a thin black stream of smoke. To even the most unsophisticated observer, it was clear: the Italians were blocked. Now the cardinals—openly and to their own amazement—began to explore a radical idea.

A Polish pope! As unthinkable as it might have been, in retrospect, Wojtyla had been meticulously, if not divinely, groomed for the October 1978 election. Once the cardinals began to accept the notion of a non-Italian papacy, they increasingly began to see in Wojtyla precisely what the Church needed: he was young, pastoral, brilliant, and deeply spiritual. Though he was from a remote Eastern Bloc country, he had traveled all over the world. He had humble roots, but had earned doctorates in theology and philosophy at prestigious universities. He had run parishes and the archdiocese of Krakow with enormous energy and imagination. He had dealt with the Communists and understood Cold War politics. Amazingly, he spoke eight languages fluently.

Overnight, Wojtyla appeared less as the fallback candidate and more as a man who was uniquely, if not providentially, suited for primacy among the successors to the Apostles.

On the second day, the cardinals voted again. The momentum for Wojtyla had built steadily, almost from nowhere, like a giant waking up from a long nap. On the third ballot, Wojtyla looked strong. On the fourth ballot, when it became clear that the impossible was happening, Wojtyla buried his face in his hands. Once the number of votes passed seventy-five, he collected himself and began writing what would be his famous greeting to the unsuspecting thousands gathered in St. Peter's Square.

On October 16, 1978, Cardinal Wojtyla, age fifty-eight, was elected the 264th successor to St. Peter, bishop of Rome, Patriarch of the West, and Pontifex Maximus of the Church Universal.

He took the name John Paul II.

WOJTYLA, THE FOREIGNER

The crowd in St. Peter's Square was getting impatient. This was its second day of waiting, praying, guessing, and, for some, wagering.

At last, white smoke appeared from the chimney.

Cardinal Pericle Felici stepped out on St. Peter's balcony and offered the traditional greeting in a moment thick with anticipation: *"Annuntio vobis gaudium magnun—habemus papam."* ("I announce to you a great joy—we have a pope.")

"Carolum Sanctae Romanae Ecclesiae Cardinalem Wojtyla—Ioannem Paulum Secundum!"

THE POPE'S CORONATION, OCTOBER 22, 1978

In Poland, streets were empty. Every man, woman, and child—even Communists with their families—were gathered before television sets to see Karol Cardinal Wojtyla crowned pope. In Chicago, the city with the world's largest Polish population, the children and grandchildren of immigrants who had been the brunt of jokes in America swelled with ancestral pride. Polish jokes were suddenly out of fashion. The boy-orphan from Wadowice was about to enter into history.

In Rome more than three hundred thousand celebrants streamed into St. Peter's Square. The coronation was a world event, so the people came in all colors, speaking in all languages. Diplomats, royalty, and politicians came, as did Rome's famous pickpockets and hawkers with their tacky papal souvenirs. Only seven weeks before, on September 3, many of these same people had been in this same square for the coronation of John Paul I, but this was a remarkably different occasion. Once again the square was a sea of flapping gold and white Vatican flags, but this time the sea was interrupted by drifts of red and white Polish flags in the fists of the twenty thousand Poles who had made their way to Rome to witness this impossible crowning. The coronation of John Paul I had been a moment of sweetness; John Paul II's coronation would be a moment of . . . suspense. The crowd was expectant, but with little idea of what to expect.

For John Paul II it would be a coronation without a crown. The new pope, like his predecessor, refused the gilded, triple-tiered tiara and accepted instead a bishop's miter, and carried a staff that was crowned—with a crucifix. As the ceremony and ritual unfolded, much as it had for centuries, Wojtyla, a

THE CROWNING: *When John Paul II was made pope, he wore no crown, only the flame-shaped miter worn by bishops. He took this cue from his predecessor, John Paul I, who also declined to wear a crown. Both pontiffs wanted to convey to the world that the days of papal luxe were over. The Holy Father is pictured here at a Roman Jubilee.*

youthful man, entered the square accompanied by the most ancient pageantry in the world. He was a trained actor, but he would not have to do much to please this audience. His first sentence was from the words of St. Peter, the first pope: "You are the living Christ!" he cried in operatic Italian. Cheers rose from the square and wafted through Rome. John Paul greeted the faithful, he spoke to his Polish brothers and sisters. But when, in the heart of his speech, he looked into the soul of each human being and said, "Be . . . not . . . afraid," a strange thing happened. Grown men in the square began to weep. Nuns buried their faces in their hands. Jaded photographers dabbed their eyes.

Maybe it was the combined effects of adrenaline and exhaustion. People had traveled for miles, some thousands of miles. They were overwrought; of course they were emotional. But for a moment, the people in St. Peter's Square, and in Jaruzelski's Poland, Pinochet's Chile, Chan's South Korea, Marcos's Philippines, and in pubs in Northern Ireland, tenement homes in Harlem, loveless homes in Grosse Pointe, the slums of Barcelona, war-torn Beirut—for a moment, the millions of human beings all over the planet who heard these words whether in person, on television, or over the radio, or whispered in an underground meeting, these millions of people were overwhelmed with hope.

"Be . . . not . . . afraid," the pope said. "Open wide the doors for Christ."

Noted French journalist André Frossard recalled that with those words in St. Peter's Square, he believed that this pope, like the first pope, might have come not from Poland, but from Galilee.

Typically, when the name of a new pope is announced, hats fly into the air, the crowd waves thousands of tiny Vatican flags, and cheers and screams can be heard throughout Rome.

A few people did clap. But, mostly, the crowd of 200,000 stood in shock. *Who?*

No one had ever heard of this man. He was not an Italian. What had God done?

Minutes passed as the crowd became restless, even irritated. Finally, at the papal balcony appeared the handsome, fit John Paul II. At nearly six feet tall, he towered over his peers. He was wearing his newly invested white robe—and a broad smile.

He began: "May Jesus Christ be praised! Dearest brothers and sisters, we are still grieved after the death of our most beloved John Paul I. And now the most eminent cardinals have called a new bishop of

FIRST PRESS CONFERENCE: *At his first press conference in Rome, the new pope fielded questions in every language. When he decided to end the session, John Paul said his good-byes and left the journalists scribbling in their notebooks. On his way out, the papal handlers informed the new pope that it was customary to offer a blessing. He ran back into the briefing room, blessed the journalists, and dashed off to his next engagement.*

THE WORLD OF THE VATICAN

To inaugurate *il Giubileo,* the Great Jubilee of 2000, Pope John Paul II will bang a silver hammer against the holy door at St. Peter's Basilica, the door will open, and the Church will usher in the coming millennium. For this moment, the Vatican will be teeming with the faithful; in all, some thirty million pilgrims are expected during the year 2000.

First-time visitors will be in awe. Vatican City is not just a city, but also a state and a country. "Vatican" was the name of the hill across the Tiber from the original city, at one time a popular graveyard, and where in fact St. Peter, the first pope, was buried in about A.D. 64. John Paul II is sovereign of this tiny universe, which consists of 108 walled acres in the middle of Rome, and fewer than five hundred citizens.

Vatican City is so small that we can count its rooms; there are a thousand of them. It also has twenty courtyards, a vegetable garden, beehives, a vineyard, the Vatican library, St. Martha's Hospice, a railway station, a post office, and barracks for the Swiss Guards, who have protected the pope since 1506. The Sistine Chapel, beautifully restored at the direction of John Paul II, is also located there, and is part of any tour of the renowned Vatican Museum. No country would be complete without commerce, and so along with the gift shops run by nuns at St. Peter's Square, there is a supermarket and a pharmacy, though they are not open to the general public. Vatican City is a media hub as well; it has its own press office, computer center (its Web page can be found at http://www.vatican.va), printing press, television station, and radio station broadcasting in thirty-two languages. There is also the esteemed *L'Osservatore Romano,* the newspaper of the Vatican, which is read throughout the world and is published daily in Italian; it is also published weekly in English, French, Spanish, German, Portuguese, and—since 1980—in Polish.

The centerpiece of the Vatican is, of course, St. Peter's Basilica. St. Peter was crucified upside down by the emperor Nero at the Vatican circus, and buried in a cemetery for paupers. Christians furtively marked the place of his grave for several centuries. In A.D. 313, at the end of the persecutions, the emperor Constantine built the first basilica directly on top of St. Peter's grave.

When Michelangelo was charged with building a new basilica, he constructed the dome so that it would peak precisely over the site of St. Peter's tomb. Archeological excavations, initiated by Pius XII and completed by Paul VI, located what clearly appears to be the authentic bones of the Apostle. (Paul VI confirmed the discovery on June 28, 1978: "Yes, the historical proof not only of St. Peter's tomb but even of his most venerated human remains has been uncovered. Peter is here.")

On this sacred site rests an architectural and artistic masterpiece. The initial response to St. Peter's is often awe—and frankly, confusion; at first sight, the Basilica is wandering and complex. Its majesty and subtleties and intimacies are impossible to absorb in a single viewing and so the visitor must return many times; eventually it feels comprehensible. St. Peter's Square, which is its front yard, so to speak, is designed to represent a key, as St. Peter was the one to whom Christ presented the "keys to the kingdom." Designed in 1656–57, it is the work of Gian Lorenzo Bernini. With its open space and the buildings forming a semicircle, it also presents the powerful image of open arms, a message at the core of John Paul's pontificate. The square itself holds about 120,000 people, but larger crowds have gathered there, spilling into the streets of Borgo, the nearby Roman quarter.

The Vatican is not only a tourist attraction and spiritual home to the world's one billion Roman Catholics, but, literally, the pope's home. He lives on the third and fourth floors of the Apostolic Palace, and has a bedroom, study, dining room, and a private chapel that seats about forty. In previous pontificates, popes have lived in rather dismal isolation. By contrast, John Paul II has opened his home to friends and acquaintances. This has taken a bit of getting used to: the staff is still sometimes surprised to find children with their parents in the private chapel, old friends from Poland in the dining room. But this pope has never kept people at a distance. Every day John Paul spends breakfast and lunch with visitors: friends, clergy, intellectuals, or scholars. Dinners are more often with members of the Curia, many times with Cardinal Camillo Ruini, Vicar General of the Pope for Rome, and Vatican spokesperson Dr. Joaquin Navarro-Valls. When John Paul eats, he does so with gusto, and occasionally he will have a glass or two of wine made from the Vatican vineyards in Castel Gandolfo, the papal villa up on the hills called Roman Castle. He prefers Polish food, but also appreciates Italian cuisine, and most meals for guests are some sort of combination of the two.

In previous times, popes had a staff member assigned to literally every papal function—from getting a hand-kerchief for the pope's sneeze to pouring his tea. This has changed dramatically over the years; since John XXIII and Paul VI, Roman pomp has been pared away, and with John Paul II's papacy, the number of attendants has dwindled to just a handful.

The Holy Father's right arm is papal secretary Stanislaw Dziwisz. The Holy Father met Stanislaw in the 1950s when he was assigned to accompany the future pope on a somewhat perilous ski outing. Stanislaw was a gifted student and a brilliant skier, and became John Paul's secretary in 1965. He is said to be warm and deferential, and constantly at the Holy Father's side. Other important staff members include U.S. archbishop James Michael Harvey, who among many other things manages third-floor audiences for the pope, and six nuns from Poland, who tend to the papal apartment, cook, arrange flowers, and keep the Holy Father's home in good order.

AT TABLE: *The new pope loved company. Previous pontiffs generally dined alone, but Wojtyla always shares his simple Polish-Italian meals with others. Papal Private Secretary Stanislaw Dziwisz, who has served John Paul II for more than thirty years, is pictured at the head of the table facing the camera.*

Rome. They have called him from a far country—far—but always so close through the communion in the Christian faith and tradition. . . ."

In flawless Italian, he continued: "I do not know whether I can explain myself well in your—our—Italian language." (Some laughter and scattered applause from the crowd.) "If I make a mistake, you will correct me." (More laughter and louder applause.) "And so I present myself to you all to confess our common faith, our hope and our confidence in the Mother of Christ and of the Church and also to start anew on this road of history and of the Church, with the help of God and the help of men." (Applause throughout the entire square.)

By now John Paul II's papal handlers were signaling him to keep his remarks brief. He waved them off and continued. When he finished, thousands of well-wishers in St. Peter's cheered wildly.

Whoever this foreigner was, to the people of Rome, he had just passed the test.

KEEPING UP WITH JOHN PAUL II

On his first official day as pope, John Paul II said Mass for the cardinals in the Sistine Chapel. He went to the hospital to visit his friend Bishop Deskur, who was now paralyzed. And he drove the papal handlers crazy.

Traditionally, the Vatican's "handlers" provide new popes with an ongoing tutorial on papal duties and responsibilities and protocol. They patiently brief the pope on his agenda: meetings, conferences, ceremonials, and obligatory audiences. They sort his mail and establish his priorities. They coach him, and by coaching him, they control him. But John Paul II was not a particularly willing student.

From his first address to the well-wishers at St. Peter's Square, John Paul II indicated that he would be doing things his way. When he went

FOR POLES, IT WAS A MIRACLE: *The Poles were stunned when Karol Wojtyla, the archbishop of Krakow, was elected pope. While the faithful gathered to celebrate, the Communists called emergency meetings to see what the implications would be for the future of Poland.*

ON THE MOVE: *The papal staff was unprepared for the energy and intensity of the new pope. Flitting from meeting to meeting, he worked eighteen- to twenty-hour days. Here he flies down the papal corridor with his close aides.*

THE EARLY DAYS: *At first people projected onto John Paul II whatever it was they wanted him to be. As his views on a variety of subjects became better known, he would surprise the world with his blend of orthodox Catholic doctrine, modern political savvy, compassion for the disenfranchised, and fierce opposition to war.*

out into crowds, he was a security nightmare, shaking hands, blessing babies, embracing the elderly and infirm. If he wanted to visit a friend, he just did. To the horror of his communications office, he would hold impromptu press conferences, and answer questions in eight different languages, making him impossible to keep up with. The handlers were accustomed to sedentary gentlemen, but John Paul II had a teenager's energy—and a genius's ability to focus—and would schedule meetings all afternoon, sometimes more than one at a time, bounding from room to room, handling them all.

Unlike most of the popes before him, he fully embraced his role as Bishop of Rome, and took on the concerns of his new diocese with the same enthusiasm he had shown in Krakow. His disdained false formality; his handlers would strike out the "I's" and "my's" in his writing and replace them with the royal "we's" and "our's" and he would change them right back, until finally they just gave up.

Unlike his predecessors, John Paul II did not prefer silent meals in the papal quarters, but meals with friends, priest acquaintances, foreign guests. He was not interested in lavish Italian dinners, but simple Polish food, which would be prepared by Polish nuns. His first night in the Vatican, he hosted a "Farewell to the Motherland" party for all of his Polish friends in Rome. (Jerzy Kluger, his boyhood friend from Wadowice, and his wife were among the first guests to be seated.) The Vatican was reeling.

John Paul II's papacy would continue just as it began: as a surprise. He would surprise the papal staff, who frankly could not keep up with him. He would surprise liberals by tightening discipline on the clergy of the Church. He would surprise conservatives with his heartfelt pacifism and ecumenism. He would surprise the Romans by being a more hands-on bishop than any Italian in recent memory.

The only ones who would not be surprised were the people of his beloved homeland.

Actually, the people of Poland were in shock. In its long and difficult history, Poland has not generated many famous sons. So it is hard to imagine what Poland was like on October 16, 1978, the evening it was announced to the world that the College of Cardinals had chosen Karol Wojtyla, the archbishop of Krakow, to reign as Holy Father to

AT HOME IN THE PAPACY: *John Paul II moved into the papacy with energy and grace. In mere weeks, it seemed as though he had always been pope.*

THE WORLD'S SHEPHERD: *John Paul II took the first of hundreds of papal trips on Alitalia just weeks after his election. He has spent nearly a fifth of his papacy outside of Italy, visiting the world's one billion Roman Catholics.*

the world's one billion Roman Catholics.

The politically savvy—Communists and Polish freedom fighters alike—understood at once that for Poland the consequences would be enormous. The Communists, who had unwittingly done as much as anyone to advance Wojtyla's career, knew they were in trouble. The secret police issued an order that all the files they had on Wojtyla be located and hidden so foreign journalists would never find any evidence that Wojtyla was critical of the government. Government officials met to discuss everything they knew about the man, whom they now realized had become Poland's unofficial head of state.

The freedom fighters also began to hide documents. Father Andrzej Bardecki, an editor of *Tygodnik Powszechny,* had hundreds of articles written by the new pope, and he knew that the world would now want to read every word. The very night Wojtyla was made pope, Bardecki laboriously gathered everything Wojtyla had ever penned, under his own name and his various pseudonyms. Eventually his work would be spirited out of the country.

From the very beginning, it was clear that John Paul's papacy was going to complicate matters enormously. The days of Pope Paul VI's *Ostpolitik* were over. The Polish government knew that John Paul II was going to put all his power and prestige into ridding his country of Communism, but they also knew it would be political suicide to be anything but gracious at this point. To the disgust of their Soviet bosses, they issued John Paul II a note of congratulations. After the solemn beginning of his papal ministry in St. Peter's Square, broadcast worldwide and viewed by virtually every Pole alive, the government instigated a blackout on activities in Rome. John Paul II countered without hesitation, asking Vatican Radio to transmit Sunday Mass directly into Poland every week, often with his personal messages to Poles. With every Polish car tuned to the radio, the blackout was a clumsy and humiliating failure.

The next inevitable order of business would be a papal visit to Poland. Just thinking about it threw the Communists into complete disarray.

CASAROLI BECOMES SECRETARY OF STATE: *Early in his papacy, John Paul II named Cardinal Casaroli as his new secretary of state. Casaroli was a veteran and a Vatican insider, from the Ostpolitik school of relations with the Soviets. After Casaroli retired, John Paul named his colleague Cardinal Sodano to the position, where he remains today.*

THE TRAVELS BEGIN

John Paul II did not need time to settle into the papacy. When he sent for his belongings they consisted only of a couple of boxes of books. With the death of Cardinal Jean Villot, he appointed Archbishop Agostino Casaroli, a veteran Vatican insider, to be his secretary of state. He immediately began writing an encyclical, *Redemptor Hominis* (Redeemer of Man), which was an amalgam of his thinking on human rights and morality. He also issued a paper condemning racism, and issued a call for worldwide disarmament.

And of course, he traveled. In January 1979 Pope John Paul II took his first trip abroad, to Latin America for the Conference of Latin American Bishops, a meeting held once a decade. It promised to be a

TERRA FIRMA: *On John Paul's first papal trip, he initiated the practice of getting on his knees and kissing the earth of the country he visited. He blessed the people of each country in this manner as long as he was physically able. Now that he cannot perform this blessing on the ground, a bowl of the soil from the country is lifted to him. He is pictured here in the Ivory Coast.*

THE FIRST CROWDS: *From the beginning, crowds were drawn to John Paul II in staggering numbers. On his first trip to Mexico, hundreds of thousands of people took to the streets to catch just a glimpse of El Papa.*

hugely controversial gathering. Several months earlier John Paul I had been asked to attend but declined. The Curia suggested that John Paul II decline as well, but instead he asked for a Spanish tutor, and told everyone to start packing.

Thus, on an Alitalia jetliner filled with his entourage and fifty international journalists and photographers (who paid their own way), the new pope initiated what would be the first of a long series of papal trips outside Italy. When he landed in Santo Domingo, deplaned, and kissed the ground in his brilliant white robe, John Paul II gave the world his first act of spiritual theater. He would bless each country he visited, on his knees, with a kiss, as long as he was physically able.

The trip to Latin America endeared the pope to his flock, but left the bishops somewhat disquieted. For centuries, Latin American bishops had taken a medieval, fatalistic view of economics: one was born into certain circumstances, rich or poor, and accepted it. As a result, while

THE HEALING: CATHOLICS AND JEWS

"I have an attitude of community, of communal feelings about Jews."

—POPE JOHN PAUL II, 1994

Regina Reisenfeld had made the long journey from Poland to see the pope. It had been some fifty years since she last had seen him; she did not dream he would remember her. But when her compatriots from Wadowice began chanting her name, John Paul immediately asked her to join him. "You remember me?" she asked. "Of course I do," he said. "You are Ginka. We lived in the same building. How is your sister Helen?" Regina, a Jew, formerly known as Ginka Beer, reminded John Paul that her mother had died in Auschwitz and her father in the Soviet Union.

"He just looked at me and there was a deep compassion in his eyes," she later said. "He took both of my hands and for almost two minutes he blessed me and prayed before me, just holding my hands in his hands. There were thousands of people in the square, but for a few moments, there were just the two of us."

John Paul II has always had an emotional connection with his Jewish brothers and sisters. He lived in an apartment house with Jews, played on a soccer team with Jews, and many of his closest friends were Jews. This did not change as he grew.

In just a lifetime—precisely, the pope's lifetime—there has been more movement toward healing Christian-Jewish relations than ever in history. In 1965 the Second Vatican Council approved a document called "Nostra Aetate" ("In Our Age"), a landmark piece for Catholics that officially deplored the idea that Jews were to blame for the death of Christ as well as the notion that Jews should in any way be punished. The future pope was a catalyst for this document and drafted much of it himself.

Once he became pope, John Paul began taking giant steps toward bettering Catholic relations with Jews and eliminating anti-Semitism.

- In February 1981 he visited with Elio Toaff, the Chief Rabbi of Rome, the first time the bishop of Rome and a Roman rabbi ever met.

COMING TOGETHER: *More than anyone in memory, Pope John Paul has sought to heal Christian relations with Jews, in persistent, but bold steps. He is here with Chief Rabbi of Israel, Yisrael Meir Lau, in Castel Gandolfo.*

- In 1986 he became the first pope to visit the Synagogue of Rome, the first pope to set foot inside a Jewish place of worship since St. Peter.

- On September 13, 1993, the Vatican officially established diplomatic relations with the already recognized state of Israel.

- In 1997 he held a ceremony at the Vatican in honor of fifty years of Israel's statehood.

- In 1999 in St. Louis, as on numerous occasions, he asked a local rabbi to read from Scripture.

- For twenty years, in every major city he visited, he asked for an audience with local Jewish leaders.

In 1987 the pope created a Vatican commission to review Catholic-Jewish relations. In 1998 a solemn document was issued, "We Remember: A Reflection on the Shoah," confessing inertia on the part of Catholics during the Holocaust and directing Catholics to repent for sins of commission and omission. For the coming millennium, John Paul may offer a *mea culpa* to Jews and a personal plea for the end of anti-Semitism.

JUAN PABLO: *In Mexico the faithful screamed with joy when they saw John Paul wearing a straw hat.*

the clergy tended to the spiritual needs of the poor, they devoted little time to advancing the poor's economic lot in life. This had changed. A new religious movement had developed: Liberation Theology, which made economic and social justice central to the priests' responsibilities, aligning priests with the plight of the poor, and pitting them against the military and the wealthy. The results were worse than mixed. Encouraged by the politicized priests to demand their rights, the downtrodden had suffered even more repression and abuse. Priests were being arrested and brutalized all over Central and South America. Some bishops, who were seduced by left-leaning economic practices, found themselves in many cases advocating the replacement of dictatorships with Marxists. Once John Paul II concluded the movement was Marxist in effect if not in origin, he wanted the Church to have nothing to do with it.

In the conference in Puebla, Mexico, he came down hard on the

GATHERING IN MEXICO:
*John Paul has said, "The
vocation to love . . . is the
origin of all vocations in life."
Overall the number of
vocations to the priesthood
has declined, though the
devotion and enthusiasm of
new priests, nuns, and monks
under John Paul's leadership
is remarkable. In Mexico
these nuns came to celebrate
Mass with the Holy Father.*

bishops, scolding them for reducing the priesthood to political
activism. Rather than applauding the clergy in their fight for human
rights—as he did so vociferously in Poland—he essentially advised
priests to stay out of politics. Uncharacteristically, he did not even
defend the rights of the poor. In Mexico, where the press had a relatively large measure of freedom, he was criticized roundly. He took the
criticism seriously, and amended his initial statements, ultimately
acknowledging the problem of economic injustice without endorsing
the bishops' solution. Toward the end of the conference he was sound-
ing rather like his old self again. He did not approve of Liberation
Theology (or anything even tangentially aligned with Marxism) but he
did call for an end to the abuse of migrant workers, for agricultural
reforms, and for worker rights. He would offer himself to the workers
as their spokesperson for human rights: "The pope wants to be your
voice, the voice of those who cannot speak or who are silenced; the

defender of the oppressed, who have the right to able assistance, not mere crumbs of justice."

Ultimately, the Latin bishops created a report that blamed both dictatorships (many of them supported by the United States) and Marxism for their peoples' economic woes.

POLAND: THE FIRST VISIT

While John Paul II was touring Latin America, Poland was knee-deep in papal-visit politics. The Communists knew John Paul II wanted to visit as soon as possible, they knew the people wanted to see him sooner than possible, and they also knew that no matter how they responded, they had a big problem. If the government permitted a visit, it might stir the country into a freedom frenzy. If the government forbade the pope to come, there would be an all-out rebellion. To make matters worse, the whole world would be watching for signs of weakness or heavy-handedness.

The pope did not overplay his hand. With the confidence of a player who knows he's already won, he treated the Communists with courtesy. The government, however, was subject to enormous pressure from the Soviets. Leonid Brezhnev insisted that Poland deny the new pope entry just as it had denied Pope Paul VI entry for Poland's millennium celebration in 1966. First Secretary Gierek reminded him that there was a slight difference: this new pope was Polish. Gierek was between a rock, so to speak, and a hard place.

In the end, Primate Wyszynski and First Secretary Gierek negotiated the matter. Initially the pope wanted to make the visit on the nine hundredth anniversary of St. Stanislaw's martyrdom in May. Knowing that St. Stanislaw was political gunpowder (he was killed in 1079 by excommunicated Polish king Boleslaw), Gierek rejected the idea of a May trip but agreed to a nine-day tour in June. Wyszynski issued the formal invitation to the pontiff, and it was reinforced with a politely worded "second" from the Polish government.

TO POLAND: *John Paul was determined to visit Poland early in his papacy, placing the Communists in a dilemma. If they were too hospitable, it would be a sign of weakness. If they forbade his visit, there would be rioting in the streets. Ultimately, they approved a nine-day trip, and when John Paul II descended from his plane to the Motherland, the crowds went wild.*

THE ROAD OF LOVE:
Before the pope came for his first visit to Poland in 1979, the people lovingly lined his path with fresh flowers in welcome, as on this street in Krakow. Many other nations would follow this practice. With few exceptions, the pope has received a glorious welcome wherever he has traveled in the world.

And so on June 2, 1979, Pope John Paul II landed in Warsaw and, as was his custom, he deplaned, kneeled, and kissed the Polish soil.

The Poles went wild.

In all, some ten million Poles—almost a third of the country—came to see him and worship with him. Not surprisingly, everywhere he went he referred to the heroic deeds of St. Stanislaw, "patron of moral order in our Motherland." For nine glorious days, Poles felt the sensation of freedom. They sensed possibilities. And perhaps most important, they realized they were not alone. One by one, as they peeked out of their homes and apartments and ventured into the streets to pray and sing and cheer, they realized that they were not isolated individuals—but a mighty band of millions. They had protection: a pope! John Paul spent every waking moment preaching and visiting with his people. He toured the places of his childhood and his university years and shared sentimental stories with the crowds.

It was a dazzling, dizzying tour, and when he left, the Poles, who were on the brink of economic and political disaster, were unchanged except for one thing. For the first time in generations, they had hope.

The Poles were not the only ones smitten with the new pope. From the moment he greeted the Italians at St. Peter's Square, John Paul II made a powerful connection with Catholics and non-Catholics alike. Even the media was intrigued. John Paul was telegenic and charming. He was well trained in the art of theater and diction. He could speak to people in their own language. He believed in things.

But his beliefs did not fall into neat little categories. As the world would see, his thinking was panoramic and, at first, impossible to predict. He demanded that clerics wear their collars and submit to priestly discipline. He lectured officers of the NATO war college on nonviolence, basically telling them they should change their careers and work at peace-keeping jobs. He pleaded for corporations to think ecologically and stop defiling the earth. He brushed off overpopulation theorists and talk of legitimizing artificial birth control. In his first year, he managed to delight and offend people on every end of the political and religious spectrums.

Somehow, too, the head of the world's oldest institution had managed to join the ranks of rock singers, professional athletes, royalty, and movie stars—as a bona fide international celebrity.

NEW YORK, NEW YORK

John Paul II wanted to visit the United States straightaway. In the fall of 1979, he visited cities on the East Coast and in the Midwest. Rain poured on his visits to Boston and Manhattan and Spanish Harlem, where he charmed the crowds by speaking in Spanish.

THE POLES CAME FROM EVERYWHERE: *John Paul's visits to Poland were unparalleled, drawing millions of Poles out of their fear and into the light of his presence. When he spoke to crowds like this one in Krakow, they suddenly had hope—not a passive wish, but a conviction that with spiritual and political action, things would get better.*

JOHN PAUL AND THE DEFENSE OF LIFE

"Life, especially human life, belongs only to God. For this reason, whoever attacks human life in some way attacks God Himself."

—Pope John Paul II, *Evangelium Vitae*

I n 1995 John Paul released *Evangelium Vitae*. Some observers believe the encyclical was inspired by the late Joseph Cardinal Bernardin of Chicago, who developed a theological construct to help Catholics understand the Church's position on controversial issues of the day: abortion, euthanasia, capital punishment, artificial contraception, and war. The Catholic view coalesced with a simple piece of logic, defending a "consistent ethic of life."

Bernardin's construct threw a wrench into the positions taken by a majority of Catholics. In the United States, liberal Catholics tend to *oppose* the ban on abortion, artificial birth control, and, in some instances, euthanasia but *support* the ban on capital punishment and war as a means of resolving conflict. Conservative Catholics are often *for* capital punishment and use of the military when needed, but *against* legalized abortion, artificial birth control, and euthanasia. According to Bernardin and later and more vocally the pope, both U.S. groups have it wrong. The Roman Catholic view comes down consistently on the side of life as God's province to create or to take. Thus the Church's approach is seamless: it is against artificial contraception, abortion, euthanasia, capital punishment, and war (except in *extremely* rare cases). The theological integrity of the "life" argument had always been there, but never put so plainly before.

The pope's encyclical also extended the Church's right-to-life argument to the right to a *quality* life, justifying its extensive work in social welfare, health care, and education, especially for the underprivileged, abandoned, infirm, and elderly. He also stated that the defense of life requires a wholesale condemnation of violence, in the modern "culture of death."

On life issues, the pope has defended Church teachings unequivocally, though they are often ignored. In the United States, where Catholics repre-

TO LIFE: *John Paul II has not wavered in his defense of the unborn, having developed much of the Church's theological and philosophical viewpoint through his contributions to Pope Paul VI's 1968 encyclical* Humanae Vitae.

sent nearly 25 percent of the population, 1.7 million fetuses are aborted every year, about two abortions for every five live births. Even Italy and Poland have ignored the pope's pleas to make abortion illegal.

For the pope, just as it was for Mother Teresa, abortion is the source of deep personal anguish. In 1994, when the United Nations organized a population conference in Cairo that proposed, among other things, a statement affirming the use of abortion as a legal means of population control, John Paul used all the political currency he had to bar the U.S.-backed proposition from being included. It was a mighty political contest, and the pope won. Although it was a paper victory and did not change the legal status of abortions, it was nevertheless crucial for John Paul to advance the moral argument and to protect the philosophical assumption that life is sacred. His victory provoked outrage among his opponents, but for John Paul it was a small price to pay. Once again, he had forced the world to consider its actions from a moral rather than material standpoint.

However drenched the umbrella-covered well-wishers might have been, they loved John Paul II. They clapped and cheered enthusiastically while he criticized their morals. In an increasingly feminist country, John Paul II was received unreservedly as a beloved father figure.

Still, what John Paul II sought had nothing to do with popularity. The Americans hadn't always heeded their pontiff in faraway Rome and he urgently wanted to reestablish papal authority. He would do so with uneven success. The Church in the United States had taken enormous liberties with Vatican II and the results were not good. Vocations had collapsed, mass attendance was down, and religious groups were openly rebelling against the disciplines and doctrines of the Church. John Paul hit the U.S. clergy hard. He disciplined priests teaching at Catholic universities who questioned Catholic theology. In Washington, D.C., he listened patiently to a nun's argument to allow women to be ordained as priests—and then turned her down flat. He forced priests and nuns who were running for political office to quit. If

TO NEW YORK: *John Paul wanted to reach his U.S. flock sooner rather than later, and went early in his papacy to the United States. In Harlem, he received a hero's welcome.*

the U.S. clergy anticipated any relaxation in Church discipline with this pope, they were in for a rude surprise.

While Americans loved John Paul II the man, they ignored the parts of his message that didn't suit them. In the United States the Catholic Church is so identified with its positions on artificial birth control, priestly celibacy, abortion, and homosexuality that many liberal American Catholics would judge him only on these issues—waiting to see if he would overturn Church teachings. They would be disappointed. John Paul II was not about to change Church teachings, and he wasn't interested in being well liked, a fact that the poll-driven American media would never seem to grasp.

Interestingly, at the outset, John Paul II didn't understand Americans any better than they understood him. Like many Europeans, he stereotyped the United States as shallow and gun-crazy. Over time he would amend his thinking. He would come to see Americans as unusually big-hearted—they would give gigantic sums to his charities and to help his poor. He also saw the most advanced capitalist nation as infected with materialism and disparities in wealth, and he would shake his head as he watched the infection spread to the whole world.

TOUGH LOVE FOR THE U.S.: *For the pope, liberty is a theological concept, "the measure of how much love we are capable of giving," rather than the unbridled freedom valued by most Americans. Though the pope was often openly critical of U.S. morals and the excesses of capitalism, Catholics and non-Catholics alike turned up to see him in record numbers. Here he stands before the Statue of Liberty in New York.*

THE THIRD WORLD

John Paul II looked at the African continent in somewhat the same way Americans looked at the moon in the 1960s—as the last great frontier. At the Second Vatican Council he had been captivated with the Africans he met and came to know. He had promoted many Africans, and sought intelligence on the differences in culture and practices so the Church might better serve the continent. He sought to educate himself on the internecine politics of each nation and the myriad tribes and animist religions. In May 1980 he took his first journey to Africa and toured Zaire, Congo, Kenya, Ghana, Upper Volta, and the Ivory Coast. His respect for African culture ran deep. He encour-

aged Africans not to become Westernized but to preserve their culture and "offer it as your contribution to the world." He tapped his foot to the African rhythms, and delighted in the children with their native garb. Though he was constantly reprimanding Western priests who didn't wear the traditional collar, he had no sharp words for his African clergy, who mostly wore open collars and huge crosses as signs of their priesthood. "Be yourselves," he told the Africans. "Guard against both Western materialism and Marx[ism]."

John Paul has visited the continent of Africa thirteen times during his papacy. He has named 307 African bishops and twelve African cardinals. Various cultural practices in Africa have made evangelism a complicated proposition—many Africans retain their polytheistic animistic worldview while practicing Catholicism as well—but John Paul has been very accommodating of African customs.

With no time to waste, John Paul II went to Brazil, a country he would come to love. Now he addressed the plight of the Brazilians

AFRICA'S BIG PICTURE:
"Certain African situations can not be judged by our criteria," John Paul said in 1980, when asked about his relations with African dictators. "This does not mean tolerating abuses. It means only that Africans find themselves at a different moment of history. . . . The Africans are just beginning their independence." Still, John Paul was so vehemently opposed to apartheid that he would not visit South Africa before the system changed. Here he meets with Nelson Mandela at the Vatican.

with political fervor that could barely be distinguished from the Liberation Theology he had once denounced. To prepare for the trip, John Paul had spent seven weeks studying Portuguese. He would use the language to speak forcefully about the poverty and injustice and government cruelty he saw.

He spoke before a youth rally, supporting their fight for social justice, telling them in their own language, "Do not hide your desire to transform radically those social structures you find unjust. You say, and rightly, that it is impossible to be happy if one sees that a multitude of one's brothers lack the minimum necessary. . . . When I was young, I lived by these same convictions."

When he went to Rio de Janeiro, he was overwhelmed by a slum he visited—and spontaneously gave his papal ring to the community. In São Paulo he was overcome when he saw a lawyer for the archdiocese who was scarred and crippled, the victim of a brutal attack by promilitary thugs. Everyone knew the government was to blame, and when John Paul II had him lifted in his wheelchair to the stage and embraced him publicly, hundreds of thousands of Brazilians knew the pope was also embracing their cause.

A SHIPYARD IN GDANSK

While John Paul II was in Brazil in the summer of 1980, strikes began breaking out in Poland. As usual the Poles were agitated because food prices were high and wages were low. They were weary and frustrated, but instead of wholesale grievances, they were now chasing a concrete goal. They wanted the freedom to establish independent labor unions, a longtime goal of John Paul's. The matter came to a head when workers in the Lenin Shipyard in Gdansk decided to strike on behalf of a fired employee, Anna Walentynowicz, who was just a few months short of retirement and had lost her job because she was a free union activist. The workers demanded she get her job back.

Ten years before in Gdansk, workers had been murdered in cold

blood by the government, and ghosts still haunted the town. Thus when the strikers locked themselves in the shipyard and erected a large wooden cross at its entrance, all of Poland stopped to watch. The strike was led unofficially by an out-of-work electrician named Lech Walesa. (Actually, Walesa wasn't even there at the beginning, but when he heard about it he broke through a police barricade and climbed over the shipyard fence to join the workers.) It might have been an isolated, forgotten event, but for a strange phenomenon. One by one, workers in other shipyards threw their support to the Gdansk workers. They struck—in villages, towns, and cities. The strike spread across the entire country. It was unorganized but unified. It was not religious, but all the workers involved invoked the protection of the Holy Father. Instead of weapons, they waved the papal flag. They bore the photo of their Polish pope and the Black Madonna of Czestochowa. Without plan or

SOLIDARITY: *In 1980 strikes began breaking out in Poland. Poles, emboldened by their frustrations and the spiritual protection of the Church, created the Solidarity movement.*

Within the image: SOLIDARNOŚĆ   ...żeby Polska była Polska...

LECH WALESA: *An unemployed electrician, Lech Walesa became the spokesperson for the Solidarity movement, leading the people's revolt. A devout Catholic, Walesa had been a background character until the strike at Gdansk, when he jumped over the shipyard fence and joined the strikers, who were calling for the reinstatement of a woman who had been fired for being active in the free union movement. From that point on, he unofficially and then officially rose through the ranks to leadership.*

foresight, the nonviolent movement for a national labor union erupted overnight throughout Poland. And it was given a name: Solidarity.

The formation of Solidarity, a national labor union of Poles, would be the beginning of the end of the Soviet empire.

First Secretary Gierek could not believe the news. He had just come back from the Soviet Union, having reassured Party bosses that everything in Poland was under control. The last thing he could afford was another strike—or another massacre—in a Gdansk shipyard. Privately he and his secretary of defense, General Wojciech Jaruzelski, agreed that their only option was to negotiate with the workers; they would accept almost any deal, as long as it was peaceful. Gierek immediately enlisted Primate Wyszynski, with whom he had maintained an extremely good working relationship. Gierek convinced the cardinal to plead for an immediate end to the strike. Wyszynski went public with his appeal to Poles to end the strike, thinking it was the only way to avoid bloodshed, and not grasping what was obvious to any Polish child: that the workers, for the first time, had the upper hand.

The pope, with his finely tuned political antennae, didn't echo

Wyszynski's plea to the workers, and his silence was seen as a rebuke— and as encouragement. The workers were now asking for more than Anna's job back: they wanted other jobs restored (including Walesa's), they wanted a shrine to the Poles massacred in 1970, and they wanted wage increases. As their negotiations with the government got down to brass tacks, it became obvious they had the clout to negotiate on behalf of the striking workers in *other* shipyards. The most significant gain of the day would be the right to form Solidarity, the national free labor union. The intellectual class, represented by KOR and the Catholic Intelligentsia Club, vocally backed Walesa and Solidarity, giving much-needed counsel on legal issues and contract terms. At this critical juncture John Paul II blessed the movement from Rome. Suddenly, miraculously, and nonviolently, all of Poland and the Roman Catholic Church were united on behalf of the Polish worker. The government would generate a document meeting most of the people's demands and Lech Walesa would sign it on August 31, 1980, using a fat souvenir pen from John Paul II's 1979 visit.

Like a game of dominoes, one by one all of the government-connected unions fell and reinvented themselves as offshoots of Solidarity. Solidarity's concession was that in return for its independence, it would not attempt to overthrow the Communists.

In a sense, it already had.

The next question, of course, was how far the Soviets would let things go before they sent in the tanks.

THE ASSASSIN

John Paul II was the first pope in history to meet his flock "where they lived." After his eighty-five trips abroad, no man's face on the planet is more familiar. But his flock also comes to him. Every Wednesday, when he is in Rome, the pope holds a "general audience." Visitors from all over the world make the pilgrimage to Rome just for this event. During the winter season the pope receives these pilgrims inside

St. Peter's or in the magnificent Paul VI Hall, built by Pier Luigi Nervi in 1971; when the weather warms it is held outdoors in Bernini's famous square. On a typical day, the pope blesses everyone, greeting tour groups, schoolchildren, contingents of priests and nuns. Special guests including dignitaries are seated on one side of the papal chair, protected by a simple canopy, and groups of the infirm or disabled line the other side. From his chair, the pope welcomes each block of visitors in their native tongue. But the gathering is carnival-like and huge and so the pope also rides his "popemobile" through the crowd, waving, making the sign of the cross, touching the thousands of individuals who have traveled so far to see him.

On May 13, 1981, as was his custom, John Paul II rode the popemobile through the adoring crowd in the square. It was a clear, sunny afternoon, and the pope was blessing the pilgrims in the name of the Father and of the Son and of the Holy Spirit. As the popemobile

neared the Bronze Gate that leads to the papal residence, a twenty-three-year-old Turk named Mehmet Ali Agca opened fire, just twenty feet away. A Franciscan nun grabbed the assassin and with the help of the crowd held him until police shoved through the crowd to wrestle him down.

John Paul II, severely wounded, was rushed in an ambulance to Gemelli Polyclinic of the Catholic University of the Sacred Heart. The pope, who remained conscious, prayed aloud. He had suffered bullets in the left hand, shoulder, colon, and intestine. The worst missed a primary artery by an infinitesimal fraction of an inch. The pope's long-time secretary, Monsignor Stanislaw Dziwisz, administered the last rites. After four hours of surgery, the pope forgave the man who had shot him.

Agca confessed to the assassination attempt immediately. He was well known in terrorist circles as a member of the group that had mur-

THE ATTEMPT TO KILL JOHN PAUL: *A Turk named Mehmet Ali Agca fired three bullets at John Paul just twenty feet from the popemobile. The pope collapsed, having suffered near-fatal wounds to the abdomen. He was rushed to Gemelli Polyclinic, while the world prayed for his survival.*

OUR LADY OF FATIMA:
On the one-year anniversary of the assassination attempt, John Paul visted Fatima, Portugal. As he had sustained his gunshot wound on the Feast Day of Our Lady of Fatima, at 5 P.M.—the hour the Blessed Mother appeared to three shepherd children in 1917—John Paul was convinced that Mary's intercession saved his life. When he went to Fatima, he thanked Our Lady, and placed the bullet that nearly killed him in her crown.

dered a liberal editor of the Istanbul newspaper *Milliyet*. Eighteen months earlier he had escaped from prison and had written *Milliyet* a letter stating his intention to kill the pope, whom he called the "commander of the Crusades." His threat apparently was not taken seriously. In 1984 the Italians charged Agca along with three Bulgarians and a handful of Turks with conspiracy to murder John Paul II, but two years later the supposed accomplices were acquitted for lack of evidence.

John Paul convalesced in the hospital for twenty-two days. He established a makeshift office at his bedside and con-celebrated Mass each day. He conducted the affairs of the Church. He prayed. While Italian investigators and major Western intelligence agencies scurried about in a frenzy to determine who Agca was and who was behind him, the pontiff moved on, tending the simpler, more painful reality. His gut had been ripped open. His shoulder was torn apart. He had lost the use of a finger. His work was to forgive the stranger, and to heal.

After he recovered from the assassination attempt, one of the pope's first concerns was about Poland—and the health of the primate. Wyszynski had been suffering from cancer and was in an extremely weakened state. Before the primate died, Wyszynski and John Paul spoke on the phone, and prayed together. Wyszynski recommended that Josef Cardinal Glemp be named head of the Polish church, and the pope agreed. The primate prophesied that John Paul would usher in the next millennium, a belief to which the Holy Father has clung even in his own weakened condition.

POLAND UNDER MARTIAL LAW

FORGIVING AGCA:
Ultimately, the Holy Father met with the Turkish assassin to offer forgiveness. They spoke for twenty minutes.

John Paul spent the summer recovering from his gunshot wounds, though his schedule remained onerous. Over the ensuing months it became clear that a new cast of characters would emerge to determine Poland's fate. Wyszynski had died, and Glemp was the new primate. Brezhnev had died, and the Central Committee replaced Brezhnev

with Yuri Andropov, who would be followed months later by Konstantin Chernenko.

Gierek became the scapegoat for all of Poland's woes, and after some shuffling the Central Committee chose General Jaruzelski, the former defense minister, to preside over Poland. Jaruzelski came off as a cold, impenetrable character, probably because he wore sunglasses all the time. In reality he was an emotional man. Though he was an atheist, he had been born a Catholic and was respectful of the Catholic religion. But Jaruzelski, like Gierek before him, was under tremendous pressure to dismantle Solidarity and get the country "under control." In a nation of thirty-five million, Solidarity had twelve million mem-

THE POPE IN PRAYER

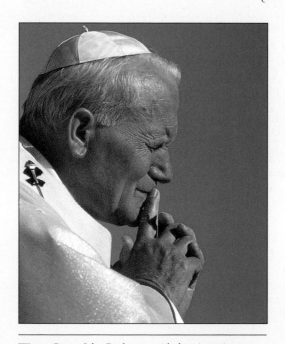

WITH GOD: *John Paul prays with deep intensity, even in the midst of crowds.*

Since the 1940s, when he was a seminarian in Nazi-occupied Krakow, John Paul has displayed enormous physical and mental energy. As a practical matter, he sleeps fewer hours than most people, usually five hours or so a night. In older age, he has added a nap to his daily routine; still, for a seventy-nine-year-old gentleman who has sustained gunshot wounds and several major surgeries and illnesses, he has extraordinary reserves and a unique ability to focus.

Many people close to the Holy Father ascribe that ability to his lifetime practice of contemplative prayer. John Paul II prays up to seven hours a day, not just in single sittings, as he does at the day's beginning, but in the midst of crowds, on the altar, in planes—virtually at all times. Indeed, when he is not centered in prayer or speaking, he often is praying the Rosary. Often you will see his lips moving: "Ave Maria, gratia plena, Dominus tecum. . . ." You will also see him cradle his forehead with his two hands. Other times he will hold his forehead with a single hand, his expression deeply intent, if not pained.

When he prays, he loses his sense of time. His assistants learned early on that if he was "missing" or late for an appointment, he could usually be found in his chapel or a quiet corner, on his knees.

bers, which was tantamount to every single *household* in Poland. The Soviets could no longer tolerate its existence. Jaruzelski had the choice of either welcoming the Soviet tanks—which were already lined up at the border—or handling the situation as best he could on his own, perhaps with the backup of martial law. He chose the latter.

Jaruzelski imposed martial law on Poland on December 13, 1981, or Twelve-Thirteen, as it would come to be known. It was a well-orchestrated affair, and it plunged Poles into a national state of gloom. Jaruzelski cut off communications and imprisoned thousands of labor leaders and militants. Strikes were banned. Lech Walesa was put under house arrest. Phones were cut off, or monitored. Poles were forbidden to leave the country.

From St. Peter's Square, Pope John Paul prayed in his weekly Wednesday audience for the freedom of his Motherland, invoking the Queen of Poland, Our Lady of Czestochowa. The people of Rome and Catholics all over the world prayed with him. His prayers, broadcast over Vatican Radio, reached the people of Poland.

The new primate, Glemp, issued a message to the nation that was so soft that the Communists used it to their advantage, and broadcast it repeatedly. The primate of Hungary suggested that Poles relent to the political reality of the situation, in other words, give up. Under house arrest, Lech Walesa lost perspective, and his bizarre response was to become grandiose.

But the intellectuals who supported Solidarity responded quickly and efficiently, understanding that martial law was essentially a war state. They began establishing communication systems and lines of command. They created secret food and supply depots, especially for families of people who were incarcerated. They called on the people to attend Mass in huge numbers, as a demonstration of resolve. From Rome, Polish expatriates and sympathetic Europeans established elaborate means to smuggle in everything from printers' ink to noodles. John Paul kept his words of encouragement flowing through the circuitous route of his weekly audiences in Rome. The pope spoke often of "solidarity" as a concept of spiritual community and fortitude. Over and again he asked the world to pray for his beloved Poland.

On December 23, 1981, President Ronald Reagan ordered a trade embargo on Poland. Pope John Paul tried to dissuade the United States

GENERAL JARUZELSKI: *Jaruzelski was the last big player in the Communist takeover of Poland. Though an atheist, he was raised as a Roman Catholic and was by his own admission a nervous wreck when he first met with the pope. Though his trademark sunglasses made him look like a frigid, impenetrable character, he actually wears sunglasses because his eyes are extremely sensitive to light.*

GREETING THE HOLY FATHER: *Wherever he went in Poland, John Paul drew millions of people who traveled day and night, hitchhiking, riding cars and buses, arriving on bicycles and by foot. The Catholic Church breathed life into the beleaguered Poles, who had suffered through Nazi and Soviet rule for decades.*

from taking the action, explaining that it would only cause more suffering, but the United States was insistent. The effects were felt almost overnight. Stores were emptied of their already meager inventory. The hospitals ran out of supplies. Polish currency was devalued. Were it not for the Catholics from Italy, France, and Belgium who sent truckloads upon truckloads of food and supplies, the Polish people literally might have starved to death. Labor unions in Europe and the AFL-CIO in the United States came to Poland's aid with funding and nonperishables. Individual Polish Americans worked feverishly to get supplies to their families. The Poles were at the mercy of Providence.

VOICE OF THE OPPRESSED

While Poland festered under its government's oppression and petty violence, John Paul became more and more concerned with arms proliferation and the deadly skirmishes that were erupting all over the world.

Having lived through Nazi occupation, Communist oppression, and an assassination attempt, the pope knew blood. He also was mindful of the Church's post–Vatican II global role as an intercessor for peace and human rights. Never again would the Roman Catholic Church be silent in the face of atrocities. John Paul's flock now lived in every corner of the planet and, in the 1980s, his pleas for dialogue and nonviolence became more urgent.

In his 1983 New Year's message, the pope noted that there had been 150 armed conflicts since World War II in what "euphemistically is called 'limited war' by those who are not directly concerned." He asked every man and woman to break down the barriers of "selfishness, aggression, and lack of understanding by carrying on a dialogue every day, in your family, your village, your neighborhood. . . . Dialogue for peace is the task of everyone."

The pope assumed the role of the world's conscience and intervened with pointed rhetoric, the well-trained symbolic gesture, or sophisticated negotiation whenever he could. More often than not he would be suspicious of the world's great powers and a blind champion of the underdog.

In 1979 President Jimmy Carter was concerned about tensions building between Chile and Argentina. The quarrel was over some obscure islands that bordered both countries, and matters had escalated to the point where it looked as if the two countries

VISIT TO ENGLAND: *In 1982 the pope's scheduled visit to England was nearly interrupted by the Falklands War. Because he believed the war was unjustified, the pope did not want to endorse either side, and a visit to England might have suggested support to England, slighting Argentina, a Catholic country. He summoned the cardinals of England and Argentina to Rome for a special Mass dedicated to peace in the Falklands, and then took off for England, a non-Catholic country, where he was well received, although the crowds were slightly smaller than anticipated.*

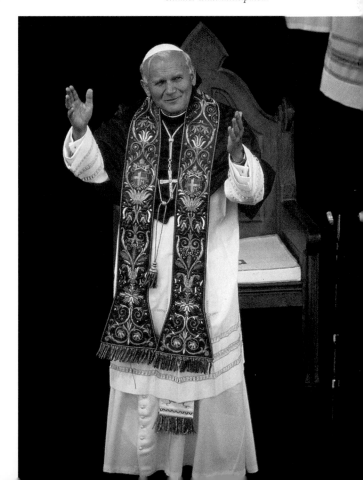

might actually go to war. Carter's people had made valiant attempts to negotiate a peace but had failed. Among others, they asked John Paul to serve as a go-between, figuring he would have at least moral authority over the two predominantly Catholic nations. With remarkable diplomatic ease, John Paul intervened just as the two countries were poised to unleash their armies. He established a dialogue and within days, the conflict was peacefully resolved.

In some cases the pope was not able to influence a conflict directly but at least served as a voice of conscience. In 1982 Argentina invaded the Falklands Island, a British protectorate, just a few weeks before the pope was scheduled to visit the United Kingdom. The British had responded by dispatching an armada. John Paul did not want to appear as a supporter of either the British or the Argentinean action, and for days considered canceling his trip. Instead he decided to get his views on record, calling immediately for a Reconciliation Mass at St. Peter's Basilica, and ordering his British cardinals and Argentinean cardinals to fly in for the occasion. When the Mass drew to a close, he announced that he would visit both England *and* Argentina—and condemned the war directly: "Whenever the strong exploit the weak, wherever great powers seek to dominate . . . there the cathedral of peace is again destroyed." In war-crazy England and Argentina, his prayers for peace got a cool reception, but he made his point.

The pope tried to preempt another, more serious border dispute between Iraq and Kuwait in 1990. The two countries were arguing over oil rights on territory they both believed to be their own. Iraq invaded Kuwait. President George Bush made the decision to intervene, though the pope beseeched the United States not to send in troops. Essentially, the pope used philosophical and theological grounds to implore the U.S. not to take action, explaining that a Gulf War invasion by the United States was immoral and did not fall into the "just war" category. The pope was so adamantly against an invasion that some observers thought he was siding with Saddam Hussein, the rancorous Iraqi dictator. In February 1991 U.S. and allied troops initiated what turned out to be a four-day war in the Gulf. His worst fears were realized: More than 100,000 drafted Iraqis were killed. An unspecified number of Americans and members of the allied forces now suffer from what is known as Gulf War syndrome.

IN GDANSK: *John Paul has made seven trips to Poland since he became pope. On his second trip, made when his country was crushed under martial law, he invigorated the resistance movement with open defiance of the Soviet authorities. John Paul reveled in the presence of his compatriots; crowds like this one held on to his every word.*

POLITICS AND RELIGION: *The resistance movement in Poland was intricately linked to the Catholic Church. The Church provided the moral and spiritual strength, while the intellectuals and labor unions provided the political strength. Invariably images of John Paul, the Blessed Mother and Child, and St. Stanislaw were mixed with political messages printed on flyers and posters, and sewn on banners.*

JOHN PAUL II: THE HOUND OF HEAVEN

ope John Paul II takes very seriously the power of his physical presence as the vicar of Christ, which is why he has traveled so many long and arduous miles. He believes that a unique transmission of Christ's love and compassion truly takes place when he is physically present to his flock. Regardless of what the faithful might be expecting—whether they are merely curious or are devout in their faith—the pope's presence produces great enthusiasm.

During his papacy John Paul II has traveled more than any leader in world history. He has visited 116 countries, and numerous countries more than once. Including his 1999 trip to Mexico and St. Louis, Missouri, he has journeyed 658,783 miles, or 2.8 times the distance of the earth to the moon.

NONSTOP: *John Paul has visited almost every country in the world that wanted him to visit.*

1979
Dominican Republic I
Mexico I
Bahamas
Poland I
Ireland

USA I
Boston
New York
Philadelphia
Des Moines
Chicago
Washington, D.C.
United Nations

Turkey

1980
Zaire I
Congo Republic
Kenya I
Ghana
Upper Volta I
Ivory Coast I
France I
Brazil I
Germany I

1981
Pakistan
Philippines I

USA II
Guam
Anchorage, Alaska

Japan

1982
Nigeria I
Benin
Gabon
Equatorial Guinea
Portugal I
Great Britain
Brazil II: Rio de
  Janeiro
Argentina I
Switzerland I
San Marino
Spain I

1983
Portugal II: Lisbon
Costa Rica
Nicaragua I
Panama
El Salvador I
Guatemala I
Honduras I
Belize
Haiti
Poland II
France II: Lourdes
Austria I

1984
USA III: Fairbanks,
  Alaska
South Korea I
Papua New Guinea I
Solomon Islands
Thailand
Switzerland II
Canada I
Spain II: Saragossa
Dominican Republic
  II
Puerto Rico

1985
Venezuela I
Ecuador
Peru I
Trinidad
Tobago
The Netherlands
Luxembourg
Belgium I
Togo
Ivory Coast II
Cameroon I
Central African
  Republic
Zaire II
Kenya II
Morocco
Switzerland III:
  Kloten
Liechtenstein

1986
India
Colombia
St. Lucia
France III

Bangladesh
Singapore
Fiji
New Zealand
Australia I
Seychelles

1987
Uruguay I
Chile
Argentina II
Germany II
Poland III

USA IV
Miami
Columbia, South
  Carolina
New Orleans
San Antonio
Phoenix
Los Angeles
Monterey, California
San Francisco
Detroit

Canada II

1988
Uruguay II
Bolivia
Peru II
Paraguay
Austria II
Zimbabwe
Botswana
Lesotho
Swaziland
Mozambique
South Africa I
France IV

1989
Madagascar
La Reunion
Zambia
Malawi
Norway
Iceland
Finland
Denmark
Sweden
Spain III
South Korea II: Seoul
Indonesia

Mauritius

1990
Cape Verde
Guinea-Bissau
Mali
Burkina Faso II
Chad
Czechoslovakia I
Mexico II
Curaçao
Malta I
Luqa
Malta II
Tanzania
Burundi
Rwanda
Ivory Coast III:
  Yamoussoukro

1991
Portugal III
Poland IV
Poland V
Hungary I
Brazil III

1992
Senegal
Gambia
Guinea
Angola
São Tomé
Principe
Dominican Republic
  III

1993
Benin II
Uganda
Sudan
Albania
Spain IV
Jamaica
Mexico III: Mérida
USA V: Denver
Lithuania
Latvia
Estonia

1994
Croatia I
Zagreb

1995
Philippines II
Papua New Guinea II
Australia II
Sri Lanka
Czech Republic II
Poland VI
Belgium II
Slovakia II
Cameroon II
South Africa II
Kenya III

USA VI
New York
United Nations
Newark, New Jersey
Baltimore

1996
Guatemala II
Nicaragua II
El Salvador II
Venezuela II
Tunisia
Slovenia
Germany III
Hungary II
France V

1997
Bosnia and
  Herzegovina
Czech Republic III
Lebanon
Poland VII
France VI
Brazil IV

1998
Cuba
Nigeria II
Austria III
Croatia II

1999
Mexico IV

USA VII: St. Louis

MARTIAL LAW: *When General Jaruzelski declared martial law, Poland became in effect a war state. No one was allowed to leave the country. Solidarity was banned. The press was destroyed. Sometimes it was not even safe to walk the streets.*

SOLIDARITY, SOLIDARITY

Pope John Paul's long-awaited second trip to Poland began June 16, 1983. Martial law had been suspended since the beginning of the year, but it had not officially ended. The prisons were still bulging with political dissidents, many of them the pope's protégés. John Paul was returning to a very different Poland from the one he visited in 1979, when he had arrived as the Polish son triumphant.

The Poles were worn to the bone. The resistance was fragmented and dispirited. The Catholic Church was allowed to operate and was the distribution mechanism for all food, medicines, and clothing for the political prisoners and their families. Stalwarts in KOR worked underground and kept communications alive, in the form of illegal tracts, newspapers, and bulletins. But the people of Poland were in a deep, national depression.

Early in the trip John Paul met with General Jaruzelski, who was a nervous wreck. Despite the fact that he was an atheist, Jaruzelski was in awe of the pope, and after the televised encounter he admitted that his knees literally had been knocking. By most accounts Jaruzelski held forth and the pope basically listened. They met for more than two hours. During their meeting John Paul extracted permission to meet with Walesa, and to tend to the faithful. His primary stop would be Czestochowa, the home of the beloved Black Madonna.

Once again the Poles flocked to John Paul. They came to Czestochowa in long processions. The roads were jammed with cars but with the high price of gasoline even more people approached on foot. The Poles were more subdued than they had been on the pope's previous visits. By the hundreds of thousands, they gathered for Mass in the open air.

John Paul, who well knew the power of words, knew that a single word could revive Poland. Surrounded by Communist guards and secret police, the faithful waited expectantly, to see if John Paul would dare to say it. And when he said "solidarity" in the open air,

A MOMENT OF UNITY: *In a historic moment, John Paul II shared the altar equally with Robert Runcie, the Archbishop of Canterbury, in a joint "Celebration of Faith."*

the people were ready. Out of shirt sleeves and skirts came roughly drawn signs and banners: SOLIDARITY! SOLIDARITY! SOLIDARITY! He used the word hundreds of times, breathing life into his people. Solidarity was no longer simply a trade union, but something much more. In Czestochowa, as they passed the government municipal building, the stream of Poles chanted softly to the Communists: *We forgive you.* With John Paul they prayed on their knees for their families, friends, political prisoners, even their nemesis, the government.

In the course of two days the pope held three Masses at Czestochowa—and more than three million people attended. They were not the cheering ecstatic crowds of his first visit, but quieter, joy-

IN ITALY: *This photograph of His Holiness was taken just before his trip to Sarajevo.*

ful, spiritual, something perhaps more—solid.

The pope visited Auschwitz again. He went to Krakow. He met with Walesa. Everywhere he went, the weary Poles were transfigured. Gently but firmly John Paul restored their dignity as human beings— and as Poles. His method was radical: by his presence, he showed them they were loved. At the end of the day, the Communists were no match for the Holy Father.

In 1985, John Paul II returned to South America. He visited Venezuela, Ecuador, Peru, and Trinidad and Tobago. Again the poverty and squalor moved the pope deeply and again he spoke out forcefully. His next trip took him to the Netherlands, Luxembourg, and Belgium. At the end of the summer he returned to Africa, the land of the future. He visited Kenya, Morocco, Togo, the Ivory Coast, Cameroon, the Republic of Central Africa, and Zaire.

The Africans adored the Holy Father, so much so that today in Kenya thousands of children, cats, and roosters are going through life with the very nonindigenous name of John Paul.

THE POPE AND NONVIOLENCE

"Christ said to Peter: 'Put your sword back into its place; for all who take the sword will perish by the sword.' And Peter understood. He understood up to his last breath that neither he nor his brothers could fight with the sword, because the kingdom to which he had been called had to be won with the power of love, and with the power of truth, and only in this way. . . . I think, dear Brothers and Sisters, that precisely at this moment we are on this very path."
—Pope John Paul II, February 23, 1980

John Paul is devoted to the strategy of nonviolence, and never was this better exemplified than in the 1980s in Poland. It took years to move the Communists out of Poland, but very little blood was shed. The slow, deliberate tactic of nonviolence worked in large part because of the self-restraint of the Poles. They never panicked. They never returned violence for violence. In his 1991 encyclical *Centesimus Annus,* he explained, "[Communism] was overcome by the nonviolent commitment of people, who, while always refusing to yield to the force of power, succeeded time after time in finding effective ways of bearing witness to the truth."

For John Paul, the "truth" is the foundation of any Christian practice. He insisted that the Poles never compromise their moral high ground even if in doing so they might gain an enormous strategic advantage. Their nonviolent approach was not about pacifism or inertia or simply "turning the other cheek"; on the contrary it was a very intense resistance to the "force of power" requiring if anything more ingenuity than common warfare. John Paul often employed symbolism and theater to communicate his message and unsettle the opponent. His active use of moral and intellectual force consistently undermined the Communist's brute tactics. The Poles ultimately triumphed, he said, "using only the weapons of truth and justice . . . trying every avenue of negotiation, dialogue, and witness to the truth, appealing to the conscience of the adversary and seeking to reawaken in him a sense of shared human dignity."

The pope has been a student of nonviolence

KINDRED SPIRITS: *Well before he was elected pope, John Paul II held Masses in Poland dedicated to the souls of the Tibetan people. As a practitioner of nonviolence the Holy Father has for decades held the highest regard for the Dalai Lama, the spiritual leader of the Tibetan people. Here they are seen holding hands during a meeting at the Vatican assembly.*

since he was young. As a young man he read everything he could by Mohandas Gandhi, and as pope he prayed at Gandhi's tomb. When he was still a bishop in Krakow, long before the Dalai Lama was well known on the international stage, he held special Masses devoted to the cause of the Tibetans, who were responding with nonviolence to the incursions of the Communist Chinese. While John Paul was under the wing of Pope Paul VI, he was surely influenced by Paul's personal anguish and frustration about the Vietnam War.

Remarkably, the pope's spiritual and intellectual grooming prepared him exquisitely for the moment he would come face to face with Communism, which, of all things, he would overcome with love.

GLASNOST AND GORBACHEV

The Soviet Union was having a serious identity crisis. Chernenko, the third Party boss in three years, had died, the last apparatchik of the Stalin era. The Politburo, seriously depleted, turned to a younger man, Mikhail Gorbachev. The new Soviet leader was shocked to discover that the seemingly impregnable Soviet state was, for all intents and purposes, bankrupt. Like John Paul, Gorbachev knew the power of words, and soon began trumpeting two words that would change his world: *perestroika,* meaning "restructuring," and *glasnost,* "openness." Basically Gorbachev intended to "restructure" the entire Soviet economy, and by the time he "left office," it was "restructured" indeed.

From the moment of Gorbachev's appointment, General Jaruzelski began fostering a relationship between Gorbachev and John Paul. It was a careful, delicate game of diplomacy: Jaruzelski would talk to each one, repeat what the other had said, and share positive references to the

other in an effort to create goodwill. Whatever Jaruzelski accomplished, Gorbachev gained immediate credibility with John Paul through his actions. In November of 1986, just after Gorbachev met with President Reagan in Iceland to discuss arms reduction, Gorbachev officially cut the strings of his Eastern Bloc puppet states. With the approval of the Politburo, he essentially told the Communists in Hungary, Czechoslovakia, Bulgaria, Yugoslavia, Poland, and elsewhere that they were on their own: "Political relations between socialist countries must be strictly based on *absolute independence.*" The Soviet Union could no longer afford to maintain their little regimes in power. It was over.

"Absolute independence." The Poles did not need a translation. Thanks to Gorbachev's *per-*

IN LAGOS: *John Paul finds Africa irresistible. He is pictured here on his 1982 visit.*

estroika, Poland, essentially, was free. Of course there would be years of transition, bogus elections, real elections, protests, posturing, and politicking with the local Communists, but the locals had never really been the problem. The problem was: now what?

Jaruzelski's team faced facts and began the first steps to set up a transitional government—a sort of civic board of directors—to move the country in the direction of democracy. As hard as some of the Communists tried to resist, there finally was a legitimate election in 1989, the first in Poland in forty years. Later Gorbachev would write, "Everything that happened in Eastern Europe in these last few years would have been impossible without the presence of this pope and without the important role—including the political role—that he played on the world stage."

While Poland's transition government was worked out, John Paul arranged for his third papal visit to the Motherland. The June 1987 visit would be less magical, even unsettling. The day-to-day struggle with the Communists was over but there was a certain uneasiness in Poland, the kind of fear that sometimes comes when you get what you pray for. John Paul's army of intellectuals had all gone different ways, and there was argument and discord about what the new Poland should look like, how the Church should relate to the state, what the new democracy should be. John Paul's idealistic vision of the people "in solidarity"—economically and spiritually—did not appear to be one of the options.

What John Paul had envisioned amounted to a very complex dream. He would hammer out his vision in voluminous encyclicals on economics and morality and theology in the next years. But whatever he wanted for Poland, it could not compete with the eventual lure of capitalism. Eastern Europe now had "opportunity" written all over it. Already investors were trying to build relationships with Poles, and

BACK IN POLAND: *The pope stands with Lech Walesa, who was ultimately elected to lead Poland, though his term was short and its results were mixed.*

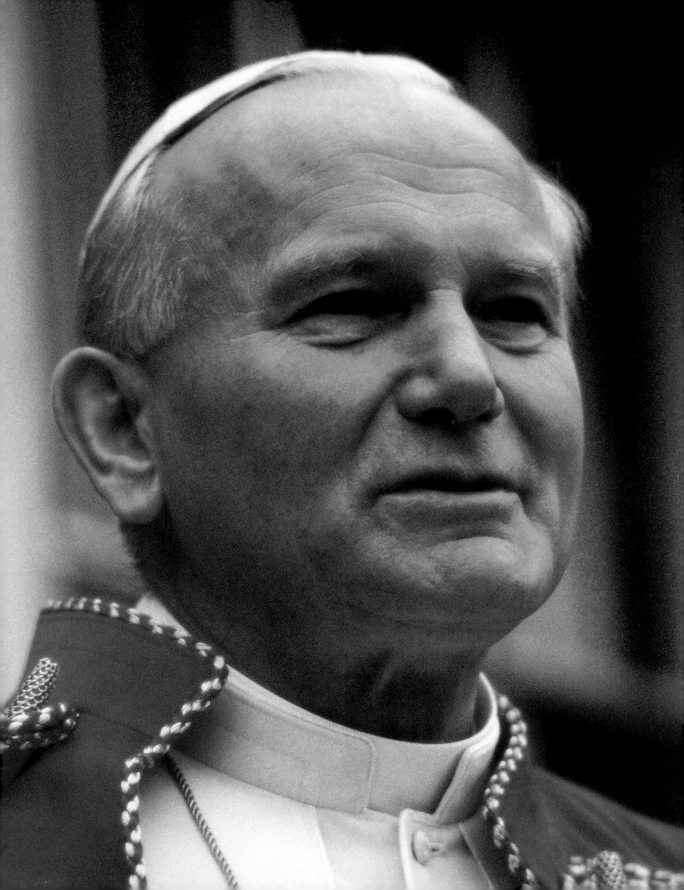

entrepreneurship was burgeoning. While the money would be slow coming, if it came at all, money was what the Poles wanted. The religious idealism John Paul had brought to his homeland would be the memory of a generation, perhaps relegated to sentiment. The pope would not be loved any less, but he would be less relevant. Even his protégés would tell him that he had not kept up with the new realities: Blue jeans. Birth control. The modern world.

By his fourth papal visit in 1991, John Paul still had the hearts of Poland, but he had lost their souls.

A LEPER COLONY: *"Nothing surpasses the greatness or dignity of the human person," the pope has said. Here he visits with victims of leprosy in the Philippines.*

NEW AGENDA: *After Poland began to shed the shackles of Communism, John Paul turned his attention to victims of other tyrannies, whether it was politics or physical suffering.*

TAKING ON THE DICTATORS

The end of Communism in Poland was the end of Communism in
Europe. By the mid-1980s the Soviet Union was in economic ruins; a
new U.S. military buildup under Reagan had proven to be more than
the tattered socialist system could bear. While Gorbachev attempted to
end the arms race, Reagan kept it going by refusing to negotiate the
Star Wars defense system. This horrified the pope, but it brought economic reality home to the Politburo. When the Soviet Union reached
the point where it could not feed its own people, let alone manage
willful countries like Poland, the Soviets came to a painful conclusion:
world domination was just too expensive.

After the Cold War ended, Poland became a clumsy sideshow of
Western decadence. Surely John Paul grieved; after all, he cared for
Poland like a father. But the pope had other child-nations too.
Amazingly, during the 1980s and 1990s, John Paul guided a long list of

nations to a semidemocratic existence, if not full freedom. His visits to a number of countries marked the turning point in their passage to social and economic liberation.

In 1981 John Paul's announcement of a trip to the Philippines forced Ferdinand Marcos to ease martial law. The pope's evident distaste for the Marcoses' excess (guests at one party were dressed in outfits to match the party decor, for instance) and his passionate statements for social justice planted a seed that was tended by Jaime Cardinal Sin. Sin ultimately was a key player in cementing the opposition to Marcos and in supporting the 1986 coup d'état that sent the Marcoses into exile. In 1995 the pope returned to Manila and was welcomed by a crowd of five million people, the largest single gathering in the history of the world.

THE POPE AND THE MAFIA

John Paul is one of history's most able practitioners of nonviolence, but he does not shy away from confrontation. In his adopted home of Italy, the pope shocked Italians by going after the Sicilian Mafia, probably the best-known nonmilitary purveyors of violence. "God said, . . . 'Don't kill!' . . . The Mafia cannot change and trample this most sacred law of God!" John Paul cried out to a crowd of Sicilians in the Valley of Temples at Agrigentum in 1993.

The pope is outraged by Mafia violence; his generally level, baritone voice quivers when he speaks of it. In 1982 and 1995 he took trips to Palermo, Sicily, campaigning against the use of violence. The Mafia retaliated: it threatened to kill the pope and killed Father Giuseppe Puglisi of Palermo and Father Giuseppe Diana of Naples, who had also dared to challenge the Mafia. Churches including San Giovanni in Laterano, the pope's cathedral, were bombed. Still the pope continued to speak out. He told Sicilians, "There is no time for sitting silently by in fearful mediocrity." The Sicilians listened. Over the years he has been credited for a huge wave of Mafia defections.

WAR ON THE MAFIA: *John Paul II can be stern. He openly—and boldly—condemned Mafia violence in his visits to Sicily. The Mafia retaliated by killing two priests and bombing St. John Lateran in Rome, but the pope's plea to stop the violence also prompted Mafia defections.*

In his 1983 trip to Central America the pope was outraged by the conditions he found in Haiti. In an outburst rare for a head of state, let alone a pope, John Paul publicly lambasted dictator Jean-Claude Duvalier and the entire ruling family for their maltreatment of the people. His denunciations fueled the cause for freedom and encouraged pressure from other nations. The Duvaliers had reigned for more than two decades. Only a few months later, they were shipped to France in exile.

South Korea is not a Catholic country; it has fewer than two million Roman Catholics, but the pope was intent on meeting them. In 1984 the Holy Father went to South Korea to commemorate the two hundredth anniversary of the arrival of Catholic missionaries there. The country was under the thumb of strongman Chun Doo Whan. With international journalists looking on, the pope welcomed young Korean dissidents to his side, giving them the stage and the freedom to speak out about government abuses. His visit energized the opposition; just thirty-six months later, free elections were held and Whan was ousted.

In 1987, before his plane even landed in Chile, the pope told reporters that dictator Pinochet had to go. He respectfully greeted the dictator at his palace and then audaciously held meetings to unify the efforts of the opposition. At each Mass he brought victims of horrifying violence and oppression and poverty on stage with him to tell their stories, mindful again of the journalists whom he had brought along. At one gathering violence broke out among hundreds of thousands of people attending an open-air Mass, and the police began throwing tear gas bombs and clubbing the people. John Paul, his eyes watering from the tear gas explosions, stood at the microphone and led the crowd in cheer: "LOVE IS STRONGER. LOVE IS STRONGER." A year and a half later, the dictator Pinochet was forced to hold a referendum on his leadership. He was overwhelmingly rejected.

FIDEL CASTRO: *Fidel Castro wanted the pope to visit Cuba after their first meeting at the Vatican. The negotiations for the pope's trip to Cuba were byzantine, but the historic 1998 visit was deemed a success by both parties. In December 1998, for the first time since 1959, Cubans were allowed to celebrate Christmas.*

ALONE WITH GOD: *Even on the altar, before crowds of millions, the pope often retreats into silent communion with God, his hand over his brow, his expression appearing pained but more likely a sign of deep concentration.*

ON THE ROAD AGAIN:
Until recently the pope was in constant motion, traveling all over the world to visit his flock. Here he greets a crowd in the United States, in Newark, New Jersey.

On occasion the pope has entered situations he knew were no-win, typified by his 1983 visit to Nicaragua. In Nicaragua priests were not being murdered by the government, as was the case in other Central American countries—they *were* the government, in this case the Sandinistas. This was precisely what the pope had feared about Liberation Theology, that it would result in individuals being more identified with a political party or government role than with their religious vocation. John Paul had asked the priests—in particular, the two Cardenal brothers, one a monk and one a Jesuit, who were cabinet members—to resign, but they had refused. Thinking he could correct the situation personally, he visited Nicaragua, only to walk into a setup. Intent on cashing in on the pope's presence, the government tried to get warm, fuzzy photographs of the pope with various Sandinistas. More sophisticated than they, the pope grimaced before cameras in the Sandinistas' presence. When they sent in hecklers to the pope's open-air Mass screaming, "We want peace! We want peace!" the pope called out in what would become his famous "Silencio! The Church is the first to promote peace."

With the Castro years coming to a close, the pope had been concerned about the transition in Cuba, and intent on enlarging religious freedom there. (Castro officially banned religion in Cuba after his ascension to power in 1959.) He had given Castro a private audience in Rome in 1996, and apparently it was a deep spiritual encounter for the dictator, who had been educated by Jesuits, and whose mother was a devout Catholic. Nevertheless, the pope's 1998 visit to Cuba took a lot of negotiation. Whenever John Paul travels to a foreign country he

NICARAGUA: *The Sandinistas in Nicaragua wanted the pope to visit to lend credibility and prestige to their own government. When he arrived, they tried to get numerous propaganda shots of the pope with Marxist leaders, but the pope—no friend of Marxism—foiled their efforts by grimacing every time photographers tried to get a good shot. At one open-air gathering Nicaraguans jeered—and John Paul called out his famous "Silencio!" quieting the unruly protesters. These nuns wait to get a look at the Holy Father amid all the turmoil.*

insists on free and direct access to the people and the media, which allows him to penetrate closed systems; Castro only reluctantly allowed this key condition. His concerns were somewhat validated. The Cuba visit was quintessential John Paul: with Communist dictator Fidel Castro sitting in the front row, he called for freedom of religion, economic justice, and liberty. Whatever price Castro paid in getting lectured by the pope was offset by the prestige he gained just from John Paul's presence. Castro was also counting on John Paul to support his plea with the United States to lift its trade embargo on Cuba.

LISTENING TO THE MESSAGE: *"Hear the cry of the poor and the oppressed in the countries and continents from which you come," the pope called out to the young people gathered at the 1993 World Youth Day.*

Critics are still assessing the trip. But in December 1998, for the first time in some forty years, Cubans were allowed to celebrate Christmas openly. In 1999 President Bill Clinton took the first step toward relaxing sanctions on Cuba.

A NEW FOE, CAPITALISM

John Paul could cross Communism and a handful of dictators off his list, but he now faced a more elusive and glamorous opponent: capitalism. While the pope supports free labor and free markets, he is as opposed to the excesses of capitalism—"savage capitalism," as he calls it—as he is to Communism. John Paul never condemned Communism on a wholesale basis; likewise he acknowledges the numerous virtues of capitalism. But when John Paul sees capitalism at work in the United States, he sees an affliction of the soul. Waste. Greed. Economic injustice. John Paul views Western consumerism almost as a mass compulsion or disorder. He believes that all exploitation—pornography, sexual promiscuity, maltreatment of workers—derives from the idea that *everything* is a commodity, even people. His criticism of capitalism is not new; from his earliest writing as a seminarian to his first trip to the United States to his support of the U.S. Bishops' 1986 controversial paper on capitalism, "Economic Justice for All: Catholic Social Teaching and the U.S. Economy," he has been warning the world about its dark side. Ultimately, the pope believes, capitalism can be a source of alienation and despair. In his encyclical *Centesimus Annus,* he put it this way, "Alienation happens when people are ensnared in a web of false and superficial gratifications rather than being helped to experience their personhood in an authentic and concrete way."

Basically, Americans have tuned him out. Still, 500,000 Americans—most of them young people in their teens and twenties—showed up in Denver in 1993 to hear the pontiff assault materialism and relativism in the Fifth Biennial World Youth Day. The media were filled with footage of their radiant faces, the endless chanting, "John Paul II, we love you,"

DENVER 1993: *"Nothing can give us a profound sense of our earthly life and stimulate us to live it as a brief, experimental state as can an inner attitude of seeing ourselves as pilgrims," the pope has said. The Holy Father has a particular affection for young people, going back to his days as a priest in Poland, where he used to take teenagers and young married couples on weekend retreats. In Denver 500,000 young people made the pilgrimage to World Youth Day to be with one another and to hear the wisdom of the seventy-two-year-old pope.*

the hundreds of thousands of attentive teenagers focused on the pope's straight talk about materialism, sex, the "culture of death," and God. It was not John Paul the nag or the scold, but John Paul the teacher. He was clear and unequivocal: "In a culture that holds that no universally valid truth is possible, nothing is absolute. Therefore, in the end, they say, objective goodness and evil no longer really matter. Good comes to mean what is pleasing or useful at a particular moment. Evil means what contradicts our subjective wishes. Each person can build a private system of values." For many of the generation Xers, it was their first lecture in theology. He did not speak down to them, or in sound bites. They listened and they cheered and they sang and they prayed. It was an extraordinary spectacle: in the most materialistic, self-indulgent country in the world, young people, questing for more, were listening—rapt—to the ancient teachings of a white-haired pope.

John Paul's inspiration for World Youth Day grew from Paul VI's twelve Palm Sunday Youth Days. Since the early days in Krakow, John

THE PRIESTHOOD: *When it comes to Church teachings, the pope has taken seriously his responsibility to uphold and defend Church doctrine. Priests here are being ordained at the Basilica of St. Peter's. The pope does not consider the ordination of female priests a possibility.*

HIS OWN VIEW: *The pope looks at the world in a way that has confounded his critics, who fall into liberal and conservative categories. But his view is consistent; it is, in a word, Catholic.*

BENEDICTION: *John Paul II blesses tens of thousands of well-wishers at St. Peter's Square in Rome on an Easter Sunday.*

THE NEED TO REPENT:
The pope has directed Roman Catholics to enter the next millennium having repented for their sins: "What we have done, and what we have failed to do." These deportees in Poland prayed with the pope during his 1979 visit. In particular the pope has sought to heal relations between Christians and Jews, and to that end he has done more than any single religious leader.

Paul had always had a deep affection for young people; if anything, they were his specialty. The first World Youth Day gathering was held in Rome in 1984, organized by Eduardo Francisco Cardinal Pironio, formerly the bishop of Mar de Plata, Argentina. Pironio orchestrated the marvelously successful events until his death in 1997. By 1998 World Youth Days had been held in Rome, Buenos Aires, Santiago de Compostela (Spain), Czestochowa, Denver, Manila, and Paris. The next one will be in Rome during the Great Jubilee of 2000.

CREDO: I BELIEVE

The modern world is unaccustomed to men like John Paul. He has no concern about being well liked or "selling" his ideas based on anything but the fact that they are the truth. What has confounded so many Catholics is the diversity of his positions on questions that typically fall into prescribed categories of conservative or liberal.

Among more liberal Catholics, especially in the United States and Europe, there is so much emotional and theological investment in the issues of artificial birth control, ordination of women, married priests, and homosexuality that the pope and his essentially "not now, not ever" attitude has been dismissed as a hard-lined conservative.

Among hard-line conservative Catholics there has been so much discomfort with the pope's criticism of capitalism, his commitment to ecumenism, his obsession with social and economic justice, and his condemnation of war that the conservatives often dismiss him as a sentimental European.

But there is a deep consistency running through the pope's views. They are, in a nutshell, Catholic. He believes that the truth is absolute. He believes that each and every human life is sacred. He believes in discipline and a God-centered—rather than self-centered—existence. All these assumptions directly contradict the impulses of the modern world. But they do not contradict each other.

John Paul, the great proponent of dialogue, draws the line at Church teachings. The pope will explain Church teachings but he will not subject them to critical discussion or interpretation. This has confused Catholics because politically he has established himself as a master of compromise and dialogue; why, then, does he refuse to discuss or reexamine Church teachings? A number of U.S. priests and parishioners who were clamoring for an expansion of women's roles in the Church—including the ordination of

CARDINAL RATZINGER: *One of the greatest legacies of John Paul II's pontificate is the publication of the new Catholic Universal Catechism. Cardinal Ratzinger directed the thirteen-year project, issuing the first comprehensive catechism since the edition ordered by the Council of Trent (1545–63).*

THE POPE AND WAR

When John Paul visited Japan in 1981, he asked to see Hiroshima and Nagasaki. The reality of the atomic bomb overwhelmed him, and his prayers were filled with passion and sorrow. The Japanese wept with him as he cried out—in Japanese—"Never again Hiroshima," and then, tellingly, "Never again Oswiecim."

Located some eighteen miles from where John Paul grew up in Wadowice, Oswiecim is the infamous town in Poland that the Germans named Auschwitz. Ever since he was a young man living with the horror of Nazi treatment of his Jewish friends—and the further horror of being ignored as he preached that anti-Semitism was unchristian—John Paul has been preaching almost obsessively about the evils of war and hatred. For him to link Hiroshima with Auschwitz might have confused the Japanese, but reveals clearly the depth of his personal anguish about the heinous excesses of World War II.

Nor has the pope been silent on the matter of nuclear weapons. Throughout his papacy he has called for worldwide disarmament and a ban on nuclear weapons. He has repeatedly encouraged young people in Europe to protest against nuclear arms. In 1982, to the consternation of the U.S. government, he sent Vatican representatives to Moscow to an antinuclear conference. In 1985, in his speech to the faithful on New Year's Day, he condemned the idea of the Star Wars defense system.

Repeatedly, whether his counsel was sought or not, the pope has articulated the Church's position on every military skirmish, intervention, attack, and war in the past two decades. In the case of the Gulf War, he went so far as to explain in theological terms how it was unjustifiable, expressing his doubt, publicly, that U.S. military intervention fell into the category of "just war." "The needs of humanity today require us to proceed resolutely toward the absolute banning of war and the cultivation of peace as a supreme good to which all programs and strategies must be subordinated," the pope stated, before the United States attacked Iraq in 1991, an act of war he considered to be immoral.

NEVER FORGET: *John Paul deplores violence and war, and was profoundly affected by the horrors endured by his fellow Poles under the Nazis and the Soviets. He is seen here praying at the Wall of Death in Auschwitz, just a few miles from where he grew up, where thousands of Jews were killed during World War II.*

The pope is particularly grieved when war is waged in the name of religion. He has sent secret emissaries and extended personal diplomacy to many hotspots involving religious issues, declaring, "Religion is not and must not become a pretext for conflict, particularly when religious, cultural, and ethnic identity coincide. . . . Religion and peace go together; to wage war in the name of religion is a blatant contradiction." He has called for the Church to engage in a historic examination of conscience about its excesses in waging war in the name of Christ, a practice he finds incompatible with Christ's message of love.

women as priests—were jarred by John Paul's reaction, which was basically to say, "Never." Likewise, when priests teaching at Catholic universities were suggesting there was room for new thinking on artificial birth control, homosexuality, and priestly orders, they were fired. "Dissent from Church doctrine remains what it is, dissent; as such it may not be proposed or received on an equal footing with the Church's authentic teaching," the pope told U.S. bishops.

Many observers argue a practical point in John Paul's defense, namely that the preservation and unity in Church teachings is crucial now because the Roman Catholic Church is going through a major upheaval. For some two thousand years the Church has been a Western European institution but as early as during the reign of the next pope, it will be geographically catholic—universal—and dominated by Spanish-speaking and African countries. With the coming transformation in the Church population, it is crucial that the institution and its teachings remain intact.

But John Paul's concern is not about being practical in a moment of tumultuous change. His belief is that the truth is absolute, whether it is inconvenient, unpopular, or even so difficult to accept that people choose to ignore it, or run away from it. His role as pope is to defend the ancient magisterium of the Catholic tradition, and he has done so with eloquence and passion.

GALILEO: *The pope broke historic ground when he issued a formal apology to Galileo, the seventeenth-century astronomer who was tried by the Church for his thesis that the earth revolves around the sun. The pope believes deeply in the importance of science and meets with scientists routinely for updates on new theories and developments.*

In obeisance to the Truth, John Paul believes the Church humbly must admit its error. During his papacy, the pope has broken extraordinary ground in admitting error committed by members of the Church. This relates not to teachings and means of sanctification of the Church, but to discretionary actions taken by individual members of the Church as a matter of free will. John Paul believes it is important for the soul of the Church to formally acknowledge error, admit mistakes, and do penance if appropriate, acknowledging that while the apostolic Church is sanctified, its individuals—from popes to clergy to lay people—certainly can and have erred and sinned. In a

ADAGIO: *The pope is slower and more emotional now, and can easily be provoked to tears at hearing of injustice, suffering, or loss. But he doggedly pursues his dream for a "Civilization of Love."*

IN LOVE WITH CREATION: *Though elderly and in constant pain, John Paul still is refreshed by nature. His doctors begrudgingly allow him to take short hikes in the Italian mountains.*

stunning move on the one hundredth anniversary of Albert Einstein's birth, the pope ordered the Church to do a complete study of its handling of the infamous trial of Galileo Galilei. In 1633 Galileo was tried by the Church for his thesis that the earth revolves around the sun, as opposed to the previously held notion that the earth was the center of the universe, which was thought to dovetail with the Creation theory. While the Church did acknowledge a hundred or so years later that Galileo was right, it never acknowledged that the Church was wrong, a subtlety that is crucial before God.

Perhaps even more amazing, in 1994 John Paul called Catholics to participate in a worldwide examination of conscience for all of the errors and excesses committed by members of the Church in the name of Christ. The pope wants all Catholics to repent for these sins, "for what we have done and what we have failed to do." He appointed a

BEARING THE BURDEN

"Before Christ I renew my vow to serve the Church as long as He wishes, giving myself up completely to His Holy Will. I leave the decision on how He will free me from this service entirely up to Him."
—Pope John Paul II, 1998

The pope does not fuss about his health. He bears his suffering quietly and receives it as a gift from God, a chance to love. He refuses routine tests and medical care, perhaps in a kind of spiritual abandonment. When friends and staff implore him to slow down he replies, "We have the whole of eternity to rest!"

Clearly he knows that his days are coming to an end, though he desires to be alive when the Church ushers in the Great Jubilee 2000 and has detailed plans for the celebration, whether he is able to participate or not.

When he was elected pope, John Paul II exuded vitality. He was strong, athletic, handsome, and tanned, standing tall at nearly 6 feet and weighing 170 pounds. His physical persona, coupled with his intelligence and warmth, was captivating. Now John Paul is very stooped and rounded, and his countenance is dull. His eyes are not always expressive. He shakes with tremors that are believed to be from Parkinson's disease.

He has prevailed with dignity, though the assaults on his physical being have been gruesome and painful.

•In 1981 he survived an assassination attempt in St. Peter's Square by the Turkish terrorist Mehmet Ali Agca. He lost more than three liters of blood and nearly died from the hemorrhaging caused by the bullet wound to the intestine. (The pope is so beloved that some of the physicians and surgeons repairing his wounds were said to be working through their tears.) The pope received the Anointing of the Sick before undergoing surgery. He spent three weeks "in recovery" though he never stopped working, praying, or celebrating Mass. He is a man of superior discipline. Upon regaining consciousness, his very first words concerned his evening prayer obligation: "Have we finished compline?" he asked. Upon being reassured of this, the pope proceeded to forgive the gunman.

•A week later, John Paul was overcome with a near-fatal response to the blood transfusions he had required in surgery. His fever took him from extreme chills to overpowering heat. Physicians pumped him full of antibiotics but to no effect. When the source of the difficulty was revealed through pathology reports, he was infused with vitamins and eventually recovered.

•On July 12, 1992, after completing his Sunday noon prayers with the public, the pope announced that he was going directly to Gemelli Polyclinic to have a large, orange-sized tumor removed from his lower intestine. He received the Anointing of the Sick, and the scar from the bullet wound was reopened to remove the tumor, which was later diagnosed as precancerous. Five months later, against doctor's orders, the Holy Father went skiing in the mountains near Rome.

•On November 11, 1993, John Paul dislocated his right shoulder, suffering a fracture after falling down at the end of an audience in the Hall of Benediction. He wore his arm in a sling for about a month.

•On August 28, 1994, the pope slipped in the bathroom in the papal apartment and broke a femur, requiring a hip replacement. He spent a month in recovery at the hospital. Since then his gait has been tortured, he carries a cane, and has great difficulty going up and down stairs.

•On October 8, 1996, the pope entered the hospital for an appendectomy, staying there for approximately one week.

When the pope needs serious medical care, he always goes to Policlinico Agostino Gemelli in Rome, an annex of the Faculty of Medicine of the Catholic University of the Sacred Heart of Milan. A small apartment is always kept available for him, located on the tenth floor in a quiet wing of the grand-scale building. The modest suite consists of about eight small rooms divided by a hall. For the pope there is a bedroom, dining room, small chapel, and drawing room. Across the hall are rooms for the pope's secretary, a gentleman of chamber, and two nuns who stay in attendance. This, in essence, is the pope's "family."

When he is in bed, the pope wears pajamas, often the same blue gown as all the other patients. When he is standing, he always wears his white cassock. If it is possible, he walks up and down the hall for a little exercise. Oftentimes he will take the elevator to a small roof garden, generally reserved for babies and children who are cancer patients. He visits with the children whose rooms happen to border his own apartment.

As the pope begins to recover, he will appear in public, a little at a time. On Sundays at noon he will appear at the closed window of his hospital apartment and pray the Angelus, the prayer in honor of Our Lady, and he will bless the little crowd of patients and visitors, as well as journalists, photographers, and radio and television reporters.

John Paul often relaxes and convalesces at the pope's summer residence, the Pontifical Villa at Castel Gandolfo. But he has spent so much time in the hospital he jokingly calls the Policlinico Gemelli the "third Vatican."

ON SUFFERING: *The pope has accepted his illnesses and wounds without complaint. Yet he now speaks about suffering from the heart. "Part of the law of suffering," he has written, "is that it entails loneliness for man." He is pictured here at Gemelli Polyclinic, where he has spent many weeks of his papacy convalescing.*

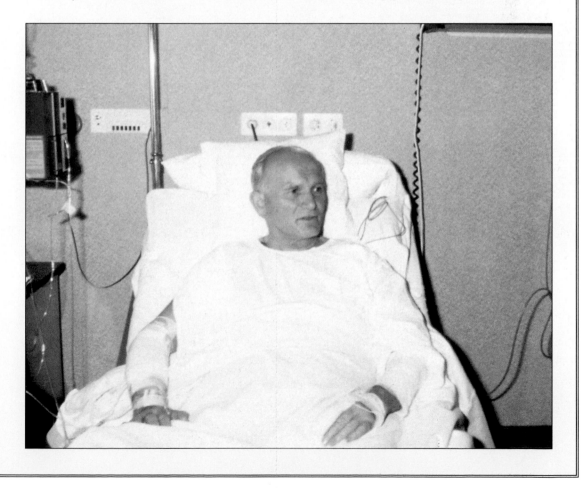

IN PRAYER: *John Paul discerned through prayer that with the coming of the new millennium it was crucial for the Church to look inward and repent for the transgressions of its members. He is pictured here in his private chapel.*

DEFENDER OF THE CHURCH: *To the dismay of many Catholics in the United States, John Paul II is inflexible in his defense of Church teachings.*

special commission to conduct a massive review, ranging from Church silence in the face of atrocities committed by the Nazis to the Spanish Inquisition to the Crusades. The first document—an apology for Catholics who failed to help Jews during the Nazi persecution—was presented in 1998. The complete *mea culpa* is to be delivered before the Church enters the next millennium.

While John Paul is not open to changes in Church teachings, he has been more open and respectful of the world's other great religions than any pope in history. In 1986 he assigned Francis Cardinal Arinze of Nigeria to organize a gathering in Assisi of leaders of all Christian denominations and of other religions—including Moslem, Jewish, Buddhist, Shinto, and Hindu—to pray for world peace. Many people, especially Italians, thought the assembly reeked of relativism, and were astonished that the pope of the "one true faith"

would give equal status to all religions. But John Paul has long sought to end divisiveness among people of good will. (On the other hand, in his best-seller *Crossing the Threshold of Hope*—which came out just before he was to visit largely Buddhist Sri Lanka—he wrote in somewhat disparaging terms about Buddhism, leaving many Buddhists throughout the world offended. The Vatican quickly amended his statements, but there was some residue.)

John Paul, the mystic, is also one of the greatest defenders of science and reason in the modern era. In 1998 John Paul released his remarkable encyclical *Fides et Ratio* (Faith and Reason). It was a philosophical shocker: a pope of the Roman Catholic Church in the post-Enlightenment era was defending the ability of the human mind to ascertain truth by reason. The encyclical is a 25,000-word entreaty to philosophers to tackle the big questions—"Who am I? Where have I come from and where am I going? Why is there evil? What is there after this life?"—and to get over the Enlightenment idea that faith and reason—"the two wings on which the human spirit rises to the contemplation of truth"—are incompatible. On the contrary, he says, any faith that is not subject to rational examination loses its validity.

The pope has dispatched not only philosophers to pursue the truth but scientists as well. "In the past, precursors of modern science fought against the Church with the slogans of Reason, Freedom, and Progress. Today, in view of the crisis . . . of science, the battlefronts have been inverted. The Church takes up the defense for reason and science. Both parties must continue listening to each other. We need each other." The pope has pointed out that for centuries religion denounced science, and then science denounced religion, but that the two, again, are compatible paths to truth. "Neither ought to assume that it forms a necessary premise for the other," he has written. The pope is a passionate autodidact when it comes to science, and is routinely updated by scientists and physicists on developments in every field.

LAST VISIT TO THE AMERICAS: *IL VECCHIO PAPA*

"He came all the way out here, in his sickness and at his age—it just means so much."
—Marisa Ruiz, 18, from Sherman, Texas

"The emotion I feel, the spirituality, the connection, is something I have never felt before. I may not be able to see the pope, but I can feel him."
—Luiz Gonzalez Contraras, 56,
after taking a two-day bus trip to see the pope,
and catching a glimpse of the back of his head

"I love the pope, I love the pope."
—Marcela Equiluz, 13,
among 120,000 Mexicans at Aztec City for
a Mass celebrated by Pope John Paul II

In January 1999 John Paul took what many believed would be his last trip to Mexico and the United States. He was stooped and suffering. When asked by a journalist what had changed since his first visit to Mexico twenty years before, he quipped, "We are all older now." Indeed, he now calls himself *il vecchio papa,* the old pope. His mind is clear, but his voice is broken and shaky. Sometimes his words cannot be clearly understood. Amazingly, however, the message he offered on this trip was as original and powerful as it ever had been.

In this last trip, the pope revealed his enormous hope and vision for the Americas. Again he called for solidarity. But this time solidarity had a new application, a different kind of interconnectedness. In Mexico he suggested that for Catholics, the divide between North and South America must end. Understanding deeply the power of semantics, he implored that henceforth, in the spiritual and political imagination of the peoples of both continents, there should be no north, no south, only . . . America. It was a radical and improbable proposal. The hint of North American custodianship was there, but he was not merely suggesting that South America was a weak twin who must be cared for. If anything, the pope sees more spiritual accomplishment among the simple peasants in Mexico than in any wealthy American suburb. Thus it was not as surprising as

many found, that John Paul also called for the bishops of the Americas to take better care of the rich. "Love for the poor must be preferential," he said, "but not exclusive. . . . The leading sectors of society have been neglected and many people have thus been estranged from the Church."

The Mexicans gathered from all over the country to listen to him, to catch a glimpse of him passing in his popemobile, to be somehow in his physical orbit. In Mexico City three million people flooded the streets to see him. As he has in the past, the pope spoke about the great need to change the "culture of death." "The time has come to banish once and for all from the continent every attack against life," he said at Mass at the Basilica of Our Lady of Guadalupe. "This is our cry: life with dignity for all."

As the pope's jet ascended over Mexico City, miles and miles of faithful Mexicans stood on rooftops and raised silver mirrors, which to *il vecchio papa* must have shone like a million stars. A radio announcer, finding it difficult to speak, said, "The pope leaves us with a ray of hope and a river of tears."

ON TO ST. LOUIS

"I'm really peaceful and calm now."
—Dr. William Svancarek, 55,
on having glimpsed the pope in St. Louis

After his five-day trip to Mexico, the pope made a special stop in St. Louis to honor his longtime friend the Reverend Justin Rigali, who was a Vatican official for thirty years before becoming archbishop of St. Louis. It was John Paul's seventh trip to the United States and this time, with the exception of a few women's groups, most of the theological and political protesters who often accompany his U.S. trips laid low. As Linda Czynski of Call to Action, a U.S. group of Catholic dissenters, put it, "Everything that has to be said has been said, and we don't expect him to change his views. This is a chance to say good-bye."

The protesters took the day off, but not John Paul. He preached his message on the culture of death, from abortion to euthanasia to capital punishment. The pope declared that America faces a time of trial today. "The conflict is between a culture that affirms, cherishes, and celebrates the gift of life and a culture that seeks to declare entire groups of human beings—the unborn, the terminally ill, the handicapped, and others considered 'unuseful'—to be outside the boundaries of legal protection." During John Paul's visit, seemingly as a courtesy, the governor of Missouri granted a temporary stay of execution to a man on death row who was convicted of killing three people. The pope spoke to the governor privately on his visit, begging for mercy on behalf of the criminal. In an unprecedented action, the governor granted a complete waiver to the convict. "It was an emotional, one-time thing," the governor explained.

The pope charmed the people of St. Louis by making reference in his speech to Mark McGwire, their home run hero, who greeted the Holy Father by kissing his ring as he entered Kiel Arena. "We Christians are always in training," John Paul said. "Freedom is not the ability to do anything we want. Rather, freedom is the ability to live responsibly with the truth of our relationship with God and with one another." The pope urged the twenty thousand youth in attendance to train for their vocation as Catholics the way McGwire and Sammy Sosa train to hit home runs. They responded with wild cheers and standing ovations—and as he said good-bye, with tears.

THE GOOD FIGHT

MAN FOR ALL SEASONS: *In the later years of his papacy, John Paul II wrote* Crossing the Threshold of Hope, *which became a* New York Times *best-seller. He also was featured on two CDs—chanting the Rosary and offering prayers—both of which rose to the top of the European charts.*

During the 1990s John Paul continued to write and produce more than three thousand homilies and speeches. He published *Crossing the Threshold of Hope,* which became a *New York Times* best-seller in 1994. A recording company produced a CD with the pope chanting the rosary in his sonorous voice; it rose to the top of European charts. He has continued to travel. By 1998 he had taken 85 pastoral trips, visited 116 foreign countries, and made 734 visits within Italy. He has appointed 83 percent of the cardinals who will be voting for the next pope—a much more intellectual, conservative, and diverse body of Church leaders than the men who had elected him. (Italy still has the largest number of cardinals, about 35 percent. The United States follows with 10 percent.) By 1999 he had blessed more than 280 saints from all over the world, and had beatified 809 candidates for possible sainthood.

On October 16, 1998, the twentieth anniversary of his papacy, some 75,000 people gathered for an open-air Mass in St. Peter's Square. More than 20,000 Poles had come for the occasion, primarily on buses. At 6:44 P.M., the precise moment twenty years before when word was delivered that Karol Wojtyla, the archbishop of Krakow, had been named pontiff, a megascreen broadcast a film clip for the crowd, reliving the historic moment. John Paul watched from his apartment window. On the screen, via live relay, the pope also heard church bells in Krakow ring in his honor.

In a humble, emotional manner, the pope asked the crowd if he had done everything he could to serve the Church's one billion souls. "Have you been a diligent and vigilant master of the faith of the Church?" he asked aloud. "Have you tried to satisfy the expectations of the faithful of the Church and also the hunger for truth that we feel in the world outside of the Church?" He asked those gathered for prayers so he might "carry out his mission . . . right to the end."

John Paul has begun to wear his suffering more visibly. After bone-replacement surgery in his hip, he began to use a cane. The surgery was not entirely a success, and he appears to be more or less in constant pain. He has survived multiple surgeries to remove a tumor on his

THE GREAT JUBILEE OF THE YEAR 2000

"The Jubilee of the Year 2000 is meant to be a great prayer of praise and thanksgiving, especially for the gift of the Incarnation of the Son of God and of the Redemption which He accomplished."
—John Paul II, *Tertio Millennio Adveniente*

In virtually every country in the modern world, time is demarcated by the birth of Jesus Christ. For Christians, the Great Jubilee of the Year 2000 is thus a unique and special moment in history. Pope John Paul II has long assigned deep significance to the Great Jubilee. As far back as his first encyclical, *Redemptor Hominis* (Redeemer of Man), written more

than twenty years ago, the Pope opened a key section with a phrase that would echo throughout his pontificate, "At the close of the second millennium . . ." He has viewed himself in large part as the pope who would usher the Church into its next temporal phase.

The Great Jubilee is an occasion for Christians to engage in deep spiritual renewal. "All of us now living on earth are . . . aware of the approach of the third millennium and . . . profoundly feel the change that is occurring in history," John Paul wrote in the encyclical *Dives in Misericordia* (Rich in Mercy). With this awareness, the Pope has called for all Christians to repent—individually and institutionally—and has even called for the Church to engage in an examination of conscience to prepare for the third millennium.

Originally, the jubilee was the practice of ancient Hebrews, who observed the occasion in increments of fifty years. At these times Hebrews would not only fast and repent, but forgive all debts and allow the land to lie fallow. This practice, a leveling of sorts, affected almost everyone. As such, for the Great Jubilee 2000, the pope has implored the wealthy nations to forgive the huge debts amassed by Third World countries throughout the world. The pope has also asked Catholics to unite with their Protestant brethren, and pray for a reconciliation of the Catholic and Orthodox Church. Additionally, he has long proposed a gathering of religious leaders from all over the world—Christians, Jews, and Muslims—for an observance in the Holy Land.

"INCARNATIONIS MYSTERIUM": THE BULL OF INDICTION

At the end of 1998 John Paul published a solemn edict, "The Bull of Indiction of the Great Jubilee of the Year 2000," under the official title *Incarnationis Mysterium* (Incarnation's Mystery). The pope decreed that the Jubilee would begin on Christmas Eve 1999 and would close on the day of the Epiphany 2001. He reviewed the three years of prayer and reflection made by Roman Catholics from 1997 to 1999 on the Most Holy Trinity: devoting each year respectively to Christ, to the Holy Spirit, and to God the Father. In the Bull he also explained the traditional elements of the Jubilee: *pilgrimage, the opening of the holy door,* and *indulgences.* To these traditional elements the pope added three new practices: *purification of memory, charity to the poor and excluded,* and *memory of the martyrs.*

The traditional elements are familiar to many people. A *pilgrimage,* to Rome or to the Holy Land (or other sacred places), reflects the sense of life as a spiritual journey. The *holy door* evokes the passage from sin to grace. With *indulgences* the repentant sinner receives remission of temporal punishment due for the sins already forgiven. The Jubilee indulgence is plenary. Only one indulgence can be obtained each day. At the penitent's choice, it can be applied either to the penitent or to the soul of a deceased.

In the "Paenitentiaria Apostolica" the Holy Father has offered guidance for Roman Catholics seeking to receive a plenary indulgence during the Jubilee. Essentially, the faithful must fulfill four requirements. First, they must be in a state of grace, having celebrated the Sacrament of Penance. Second, they must receive the Holy Eucharist on the specific day they receive the indulgence. Third, they must pray for the intentions of the pope, including in this petition at least one Our Father, one Creed, and a prayer to the Blessed Virgin Mary (e.g., a Hail Mary). Finally, the penitent is to engage in work or giving that reflects the spirit of the Jubilee. For example, make a pilgrimage either to Rome or the Holy Land, or to the local diocesan cathedral church or to the home of a person in need or difficulty. Abstain for at least one whole day from unnecessary consumptions (such as cigarettes) and donate a proportionate amount of money to the poor. Support a significant work of a religious or social nature, especially for the benefit of abandoned children, young people in trouble, the elderly in need, or foreigners in various countries seeking better living conditions. Devote a suitable portion of personal free time to activities benefiting the community.

For the Great Jubilee 2000 the pope added three new practices. *Purification of memory* calls everyone to make an act of courage and humility in recognizing the wrongs committed by all born or practicing as Christian. For the faithful this means kneeling before God to implore forgiveness for the past and present sins of the Church's sons and daughters.

Roman Catholics will also be asked to provide extra works of *charity to the poor* as part of their spiritual renewal. The pope implores the faithful to "open [their] eyes to the needs of those who are poor and excluded" and face squarely "the situation affecting vast sectors of society and casting its shadow of death upon whole peoples." The pope calls for the creation of "a new culture of international solidarity and cooperation where all—particularly the wealthy nations and the private sector—accept responsibility for an economic model that serves everyone."

Finally, His Holiness has requested that Catholics concentrate their attention on the *memory of martyrs.* Martyrs are defined as those who gave their lives for the faith. Pope John Paul II has blessed or canonized more than half the total number of "blessed" or saints in the Church's history, with a particular focus on the Church's martyrs. Of his 819 blessed and 276 saints, 603 are martyrs, and 286 of these were martyred in the twentieth century: 221 in the Spanish civil war, the others in German concentration camps, and in Africa, Asia, and Latin America. Even more modern martyrs are expected to be examined under the canonic process, since the Holy Father has authorized a special commission for new martyrs to find and gather witnesses of martyrdom unveiled after the fall of the Eastern European regimes. The pope states in the Bull, "The martyr, especially in our own days, is a sign of that greater love which sums up all other values. The believer who has seriously pondered his Christian vocation including what Revelation has to say about the possibility of martyrdom, cannot exclude it from his own life's horizon."

With the great Jubilee in the Year 2000—and its traditional and new practices—John Paul II declares a new Christian era. "I have looked toward this occasion with the sole purpose of preparing everyone to be docile to the working of the Spirit. By Holy Spirit, the inward and outward purified Church will be able to accomplish the *Civilization of Love.*" Many Roman Catholics recall Pope Paul VI's homily during Midnight Christmas Mass, at the closing of the Holy Year 1975, when he introduced the concept of the *Civilization of Love* before 300,000 in St. Peter's Square and more than a billion people watching on interconnected televison.

colon and an inflamed appendix. His left hand shakes, in a manner that suggests Parkinson's disease. His eyes have a vacant look, except when he is focused on an individual or a crowd, and then somehow the radiance penetrates whatever neurological or muscular function has been lost—and the beam is there. John Paul is not a well man. But since the shooting in 1981 he has accepted his physical suffering as part of his redemptive work. "Now that he is weakened in a world horrified by sickness and death, he thinks that the image of someone who is suffering is important to the Church," one French journalist observed. But for the millions who love this man, it is difficult to watch.

As his physical suffering is more and more difficult to bear, the pope's emotions infuse his speeches and homilies. No longer is he the stoic young man from Poland who at his mother's death muttered, "It was God's will." The pope is now given to tears at mild provocation. His tone is urgent. Perhaps, having realized he has little time left, he wants to persuade the world to listen, to heed his cautions. He wants to shake us so that we might understand.

Pope John Paul II is, to say the least, a paradox. In 1978 a man wearing a long robe, carrying a staff, and given to speaking in Latin took the modern world by storm. As God's shepherd, he touched—physically and spiritually—tens of millions of souls. He established himself as a moral leader. A poet-philosopher. A champion of human rights.

Yet he is also the son of Lieutenant Karol Wojtyla, and he likes order in his life. Today, when he is not traveling, his days follow a simple routine. He rises at 5:00 A.M. in his bedroom on the third floor of the Apostolic Palace. His room is empty except for a single bed, a desk, and two chairs. A tiny foot rug is placed beside the bed, but the floor, otherwise, is cold and wooden. The walls are unadorned except for a few religious paintings from Poland.

By 6:15 A.M. the pope is dressed and already praying in his private chapel, which houses an image of his beloved Black Madonna of Czestochowa. The papal nuns bring in flowers and the special intentions for which the pope will pray that day.

At 7 A.M. the pope celebrates a private Mass. Sometimes those in attendance are asked to join him for breakfast, whether they are friends, lucky visitors, clergy, or dignitaries. Almost everyone who has

THE PARADOX: *John Paul II, a man dressed in ceremonial robes and devoted to ancient ritual, took the modern world by storm.*

had the fortune to enter his private world describes the same experience: the pope is kindly, self-deprecating, and after a few minutes in his presence, one even "forgets" he is the pope. He listens intently, asks many questions, and is passionately curious about all subjects, especially science and physics. After breakfast, John Paul spends an hour or so writing or dictating. He reads the news summaries that are assembled for him by assistants in Angelo Cardinal Sodano's office. Once a week he reads *Tygodnik Powszechny,* the Catholic newspaper from Krakow.

On Tuesdays he invites scholars who have a specialty in a certain field: science, theology, philosophy, or politics, for example. He shares lunch with them and asks for briefings on the latest development in their fields. Otherwise, lunch is reserved for visiting bishops. Dinner is generally for friends.

The pope has a half-hour nap after lunch now, on doctor's orders. He strolls the palace for exercise, praying the Rosary or reading the breviary. His afternoons are filled with meetings and consultations. He manages more in a single afternoon than most people might attempt in a week.

On Friday nights, he meets with Joseph Cardinal Ratzinger, prefect of the Congregation for the Doctrine of the Faith. Saturday nights, the pope meets with Bernard Cardinal Gantin, head of the Congregation for the Bishops.

Each week, he prays the Stations of the Cross.

The pope goes to confession once a week, on Saturdays; an elderly Polish priest hears his confession. One Sunday or more each month, he visits a parish church in the diocese of Rome, of which he is bishop.

He does not watch television, though sometimes a soccer match might get his attention. He has seen few movies in the past years, except for *Gandhi,* which he is said to have enjoyed, *Schindler's List,* and most recently the Italian *Life Is Beautiful.* He listens to music occasionally and prefers Chopin.

He retires at 11 or 12 o'clock, and often reads. He likes the poet Ranier Maria Rilke. Most of the time he reads history, sociology, or philosophy, in the language in which it was written.

Romans strolling late at night in St. Peter's Square will point up to the papal apartment on the third floor of the Apostolic Palace. His is the light that is still burning.

LUMINE: *His window, still lit, while the world sleeps.*

"You must be strong, dear brothers and sisters. You must be strong with the strength that comes from faith. So as I depart, I ask you to accept once again your spiritual heritage . . . with faith, hope, and love. . . .

"I ask that you never despair, never grow weary, never become discouraged; that the roots from which we grow are never severed; that you keep your faith despite your weaknesses, that you always seek strength in Him; that you never lose that freedom of spirit for which He has liberated man; that you never spurn that love . . . expressed by the cross, without which human life has no roots and no meaning.

"I ask this of you."

—POPE JOHN PAUL II

SOURCES

To expand on their working knowledge of Pope John Paul II's life and works, the authors relied on numerous sources. The *Osservatore Romano* served as a principal source of written documents and statements issued by the Holy Father, and provided confirmation of dates and papal visits. In addition, *Kalendarium* provided a complete and invaluable overview of the pope's life. We consulted numerous online services and newspapers, including the *New York Times* and the *Washington Post*. We also gleaned and confirmed information via the *Tablet,* London. Among numerous texts, we read and recommend André Frossard's *Portrait of John Paul II,* Jonathan Kwitney's *Man of the Century,* and Tad Szulc's *Pope John Paul II.* The pope's writings were obviously a primary source: encyclicals, *Crossing the Threshold of Hope, Gift and Mystery,* all played a role in this presentation. Countless religious texts were also consumed in preparation for the writing of this brief treatment of the pope's life. If there are any omissions, inconsistencies, or errors, please write to the authors in care of the publisher and if at all possible, they will be corrected in future printings.

PHOTOGRAPHY CREDITS